❖❖❖ THE RECONCILING
COMMUNITY

❖❖❖ Orlando L. Tibbetts

THE RECONCILING
COMMUNITY

❖❖❖ The Judson Press, Valley Forge

THE RECONCILING COMMUNITY

Copyright © 1969
The Judson Press
Valley Forge, Pa. 19481

Bible quotations in this volume are in accordance with the Revised
Standard Version of the Bible, copyright 1946 and 1952 by the Division
of Christian Education of the National Council of the Churches of Christ
in the United States of America, and are used by permission.

Standard Book No. 8170-0415-7
Library of Congress Catalog Card No. 69-16386

Printed in the U.S.A.

To my wife, Phyllis
and our children,
Roger, Douglas, Faith, Judith

✤✤✤ PREFACE

The American Baptist state conventions of the eastern seaboard provided me with the opportunity to develop the material for this book by inviting me to deliver some lectures on church renewal at the annual missions conference at Camp Sunnybrook in Pennsylvania. Because I had just returned from an extensive visit to twelve European countries where I had looked for clues and hints about the direction the church might take, I was eager to share my impressions and to explore the concept of community by presenting these lectures.

I am most grateful to Dr. Wilbur Bloom, Executive Secretary of the Pennsylvania Baptist Convention, for his hospitality and encouragement while I delivered the lectures. I also want to thank Dr. Clarence Cranford of Washington, D.C., who was a fellow lecturer at that same conference, for his suggestion that the substance of these lectures should find their way to the printed page.

The Boston Baptist City Mission Society Board of Directors has been most supportive in permitting me the freedom to travel, learn, experiment, and write. This book is really the result of our corporate thinking and working as a mission entity amongst the churches and organizations of Boston.

I want to especially thank the City Mission Society president, Mrs. William E. Wells, who supported me while I was executive of the Society with grace, patience, humor, and prayer.

I am also grateful to the staff for their suggestions, hints, corrections, and understanding.

To Carol Freehan, my hard-working secretary, goes a great deal of credit for her meticulous work and long, extra hours of sharing her skill and energies. She and Lucille Metcalf were the real workers in making this "impossible dream" come true.

To all these, my fellow workers in the city, my family at home, and my friends in Europe, who made this book possible, my prayer is that the book may help strengthen the church we all love.

ORLANDO L. TIBBETTS

Boston, 1969

✤✤✤ CONTENTS

✤✤✤ INTRODUCTION

THIS IS A HUMAN BOOK, a warm book. Written by someone who knows what he's about, it is yet refreshingly free from jargon or any form of posturing. Yet again it has some hard things to say — for the author so obviously loves the church that he feels free to criticize it, and indeed rebuke it, from within!

The book itself is a plea for change — and it attempts to say how change can be effected. This makes it interesting. What makes it fascinating are the flesh-and-blood descriptions of people and places which have changed and are changing; and it's not just the face of the church, but it's the body of the church that is the subject matter. This is what makes it significant. For in itself the book is a work of reconciliation. And if you are like me, you will find this disturbing — and exhilarating.

It was De Chardin who claimed that we can only under-

11

stand the incarnation if we recognize its "immense simplicity." This book gives us just such an opportunity — and many will be grateful for it.

It was one of my fellow members of the Iona Community who declared that "until a person has tasted Communion as one of a small group he cannot appreciate what Communion in a large congregation is all about." This book detects and develops the implosion that is there — and everyone will be challenged by it. And how stimulating it is to be challenged, not by still another modern treatise on "what ought to be," but by this so contemporary an insight into "what is."

Dr. Tibbetts usefully shares his experience with us in an engaging way. Excitingly he also communicates his creative impatience — and doesn't stop short! Exactly because this book does not set out to impress makes it so impressive a book. It is a book that reveals to us much that we know, without knowing it! It goes a good way toward answering in this day a prayer that the Iona Community have made for years "that hidden things may be revealed to us and new ways found to touch the hearts of men."

DOUGLAS N. ALEXANDER

Iona Community House
Glasgow, Scotland

❧❧❧ LIVING IN THE TWENTY-FIRST CENTURY

WE ARE ALREADY LIVING in the dawning hours of the twenty-first century. The new era begins not with the striking of the clock at midnight, December 31, in the year 1999, but in the revolutionary days of technological advance when the patterns of life are being set for the twenty-first century and assimilated by the people of this earth — and that time is now! The population of the United States has already passed the two hundred million mark and is well on the way toward three hundred million. Soft landings have been made on the moon, and soon platform cities will be orbiting around the earth as way-stations to the moon. There will even be those who will purchase tickets from a rocket transport company to visit the moon! Defective human organs are now being replaced with organs transplanted from other human beings. The pill now saves lives and controls the coming of life; it even makes life more tolerable! Space around the earth has been united by supersonic jets as the world has entered into a new phase of development; it has become a Cosmic City! It has become what Constantinos Doxiadis, Greek educator and civic planner, calls Ecumenopolis — the final stage in the evolution of the urbanized world.

Even if we find it difficult to accept the idea of living now in the emerging twenty-first century, we must still face the awesome truth of frightening change. The most simple minded of us see the effects of superhighways, changed skylines, and multiple suburban developments which mesh with each other in a fully developed complex, urban society. Anyone of us can sit in our living room and visit Europe, Asia, Africa, or even the moon via the television set. Each of us experiences influences no man has ever before known.

Mr. Average Man may not know anything about "ecological balance" or the "morphology of the urban fringe," but he knows of the frustration he experiences while he is caught in a traffic jam day after day; of the hurt he feels when his eyes smart and his lungs are heavy from polluted air; of the bafflement that overwhelms him as he reads of, or takes part in, riots and burning cities; of the fear that grips him as he becomes more aware of a mounting crime rate and the declining safety of his own neighborhood; and most of all of the emptiness he feels as he faces this world sensing a great spiritual vacuum. He yearns for the good old days that his parents talked about when life seemed to move more easily and people seemed to know what was right and wrong. The constant news items about war and the imminence of annihilation produce a battle psychology within him which seeks an outlet for expression in escapes of pleasure and thrill seeking. Yes, Mr. Average Man is caught between the centuries; he is the baffled child in transition — not leaving the old and not quite grasping the new!

The contemporary church now finds itself in just such a time of transition. In this age Christians are challenged to carry out a redemptive task so great that the average church member recoils from facing it. But our Lord compels us to confront a world filled with masses of people caught in the web of urbanization. He bids us to participate in an exodus from the old land into the promised land with the understanding that his ways may be radically different from anything we have ever known. He would call us back to a reconsideration of man as a person; not lost in the crowds of human traffic, nor left in the midst of swarming cities, but as a person known by name, by God, and by God's people. He would call us to a new kind of evangelism which sees a man as a part of God's earth and which sees God's earth as influencing the destiny of man. Thus, issues of population explosion, density of housing, pollution of air and water, the stripping of the earth for selfish reasons, and the disorders found within our cities are all related to man's custodianship of the earth. God has put man here with responsibilities toward all that he possesses and all whom he meets.

The Bible tells us:

> The earth is the Lord's and the fulness thereof,
>   the world and those who dwell therein;
> for he has founded it upon the seas,
>   and established it upon the rivers.
> Who shall ascend the hill of the Lord?
>   And who shall stand in his holy place?
> He who has clean hands and a pure heart,
>   who does not lift up his soul to what is false,
>   and does not swear deceitfully.

Psalm 24:1-4

Because the earth is the Lord's, we who are the Christian community must become more responsible custodians of the resources which God has put at our disposal. We must become planners, projectors, improvers, designers, rulers, and if needs be, revolutionaries! As Doxiadis notes, until the eighteenth century disorder was in our jungles and order was in our cities. Now the situation is reversed, and disorder is found in the cities and is spreading outward from them. In a time when technology has risen to undreamed-of-heights, there is less adequate service to man in the total city than ever before in history. Who then shall ascend the hill of the Lord or stand in his holy place? That is, who will enter the cities where God is and join in his redemptive tasks which are related to the people whom he loves? Who can do this except the one whose hands are clean? The psalmist does not mean physical cleanliness but hands which have not been tainted by money, greed, selfishness, idleness, apathy, indifference, and coldness to the needs of those entrapped in the systems of the world. Here God is calling men to lift up their souls to what is real, good, and beautiful. He is calling his children to face the reality of earth as he intended it to be; a place where people can lift up their heads and believe in a God of love and justice; a place where people can become human, accepting themselves, each other, and the God who made them; a place where people will acknowledge that all the resources of land, hills, skies, rivers, lakes, oceans, clouds, factories, and houses are meant to bring men together into one community of peace and love and to make God known as king and sovereign of all life.

The Super-City

In order to engage in mission in today's world, we must not only accept the fact that we already live in the twenty-first century, but we must also understand the kind of century this is and will continue to be. We have referred to the fact that we are living in the Cosmic City. Doxiadis reminds us of the evolution of the city from Polis, the little Greek city, to Ecumenopolis, the universal city of tomorrow. We are already on the verge of living in Ecumenopolis though living at the Megalopolis stage. Much has been written about Megalopolis, and particularly the strip city which runs from Boston to Washington, D.C., as a continuous urban area of life. No other section of the United States has such a large and dense concentration of wealth, culture, and population. Jean Gottman says that this area is unique as it dominates the political, economic, and even cultural life of the United States.[1] Similar super-cities have been developed in Europe on both sides of the channel and the North Sea and in other parts of North and South America. The twenty-first century will see these super-cities fully developed, linked, and coordinated. Eight out of ten people will live in them and will receive all of the advantages from this kind of urban living. They will have the best schools, the best jobs, the best in culture, and the best in services. The church will have to reshape itself according to Megalopolis and the conditions it has created.

In the super-city now emerging, housing will be prefabricated and probably ordered from a catalog. Instant building will take place as helicopters lower whole rooms and floors, one on top of the other, into the densely populated city and suburban areas. The housing direction will be upward rather than outward. As costs spiral, more money will be spent on government housing programs with a large-scale rental-supplement program which will reach into even the middle class. We will learn more about housing from those in Europe who have demonstrated great imagination in planning whole areas with radically new concepts.

New cities will be planned and established both within the already existing major cities and outside those cities. Current trends indicate that suburbia will become one of the most densely populated parts of the world. Those who control the power structures of metropolitan and megalopolitan life will live in suburbia. The problems of the disadvantaged who are now found in the cities will be found in suburbia as well. The mission to inner-city slums will have to extend also into

---

[1] Jean Gottman, *Megalopolis the Urbanized Northeastern Seaboard of the U.S.* (New York: The Twentieth Century Fund, 1961), pp. 3, 4.

poverty-stricken parts of suburbia where cheap, closely-built housing units have been erected. Suburbia will in many parts of the nation become central city. The resident of tomorrow will live in one suburban area and commute to another. Employment in the suburbs will exceed employment in the cities as decentralization takes place and the super-city engulfs all the land.

The Day Boston Stopped

Boston will always remember that incredible November day when an unexpected northeast blizzard hit the area at 4 P.M. It happened because of a combination of unexpected low temperature, shifting winds, and a storm front which was supposed to have moved off across the Atlantic Ocean. The commuters heading for home were caught by a quickly freezing snow on relatively warm ground, creating a slippery condition on streets and highways that stopped 250,000 automobiles right in their tracks! Every street, artery, highway, and expressway in the metropolitan Boston area was literally jammed with automobiles. As gas tanks emptied, and trucks jack-knifed, miles upon miles of automobiles were left abandoned in the drifting snow and glassy smooth ice. Man had to surrender to the awesome power of nature's severest blows.

It is ironic that a sneak snowstorm over a great city of three million people brought immobility to the very instrument that usually keeps it moving — the automobile! Yet this unique day was not too different from other days when a combination of weather, inadequate roads, too many cars, and a lack of metropolitan rapid transit system brought about conditions which slowed men down within the city so much that today it takes twice as long to go a given distance as it took a few years ago.

The automobile has been taken for granted by modern man as the most necessary instrument for life next to the home. The Massachusetts Registry of Motor Vehicles reports that 365,000 cars enter Boston each day in the commuter jam. The increase in the population of cars, which is commensurate with the increase of the population of people, is threatening to destroy us. Each year in the city of Boston, one hundred thousand additional automobiles are added to the roads, but the roads themselves are only increased enough to take care of twenty-five thousand more annually. More and more land is being taken to accommodate the automobile. In some major cities 25 to 50 percent of the core city is now taken over for the purpose of transporting the automobile or parking it. Air pollution has become a serious problem in all major cities, and the automobile has contributed its share to this problem. Some experts predict that with an inversion of air and the lack of a good west wind over the Atlantic Ocean a time could come in Boston when the carbon monoxide of automobiles, combined with the chemicals from industrial chimneys, could cause twenty thousand people to drop dead in the streets in one day.

Every year fifty thousand people die in automobile accidents, and yet it is an incredible fact that no major church body has set up a department of automotive mission. Too little thinking is being done these days about the mobile church. With the advent of a four-day working week the automobile becomes the instrument through which shifting families will move between summer and winter homes. People will soon be spending more waking hours in their automobiles than even in their homes.

By the time the twenty-first century officially arrives, eighty-five million automobiles will be driving through networks of tunnels and over superhighways constructed at multiple levels.

A new sophisticated urbmobile guided either by a moving track or by an electronic radar device will enable people, regardless of weather or time, to get on the main highways and to go at high speeds to other parts of the country while the outside automatic, mechanized force guides them safely to their destiny. The driver will be able to sit back and read a book, play a game, or perhaps watch television. This urb-mobile will be utilized as another home on wheels with air conditioning, bathroom facilities, and comforts now unimagined.

The very mobility and rapidity of life which has been brought by the utilization of the automobile, and soon the urbmobile, will force the church to seek new ways to reach people. Professional missioners will be taught and trained to minister to a society on the move in the urbmobile.

Men on the Elevator

The concentration of population in the central city will force all building expansion to be upward. Buildings of thirty to one hundred floors will be common in all the major cities of the world. A new mode of travel will emerge as moving between floors becomes a way of life. The elevator will become the vertical urbmobile.

City planners will encourage the building of skyscrapers which will include living units on some floors, shopping centers on others, swimming pools, theaters, and other recreational facilities on still others. Schools and churches will be located on some floors for the people who live within a particular skyscraper. As the automobile has raised the question of how far a man will walk to shop, eat, play, or worship, the new question will be: How many floors will a man ride in order to do these things? Think of the implications of this vertical sky-living for the institutional church! One of the basics which will be necessary in finding ways for the church of Christ to penetrate the skyscraper will be an acceptance of the ecumenical approach to church mission and worship. Thus, as the church becomes vertically mobile, it will be brought into a closer horizontal unity. No longer will denominations be able to vie for a little piece of land to put up their individual buildings where they may worship according to their individual beliefs and doctrines. Instead, the very density of population and the nature of the housing necessary to take care of the population will compel Christians to practice a oneness which is within the purpose of God.

One Hundred-Year-Old Youths

Most people do not realize that old age is a twentieth-century phenomenon. They forget that the average life expectancy at birth in the year 1900 was only forty-seven years. Now, however, forty-seven years is considered to be middle age and the average life expectancy is seventy! By the year 2000, with scientific breakthroughs in heart disease and cancer, the average life span could be one hundred to one hundred ten years. Today there are already over fifteen thousand people living in the United States who have become centenarians. This extension of life is stimulating a continuing reevaluation of present retirement arrangements. Because of longer life spans the number of those classified as "the aging" will be 50 percent greater by the end of this century than it is now.

What will be the church's role among the aging? Retirement colonies, retirement hotels and villages will not be enough. Many more lay and clerical ministries to the aging will be needed. The church will have to form closer relationships with community organizations on a grand scale. Small active worshiping communities formed among the aging will become one of the great forces for spiritual dynamic and service in the world. At the present time the church does not know how to guide its aging in worship or in service relationships. A whole new kind of educational program will be developed. As additional time for reflection increases in one's life, the church will have one of its most opportune moments in contemporary history for dealing with people as people. Increased time means that persons will have more time to devote to building better human relationships.

Machines and Boredom

It has been said many times that a country in trouble is one that does not know what to do with its free time. With people living to be one hundred years old, and with a four-day work week brought on by automation, "moonlighting" will be a common practice among all classes and ages. At least 50 percent of all women will be working. The elderly will be reeducating themselves for new work at the retirement level. Schools will be in session all year round, and vacations will no longer be limited chiefly to the summer season. The three-to-four-day weekend will become a reality for people, and thus the whole question of leisure will come into focus. Schools, churches, and community organizations are already faced with the responsibility of educating people for leisure. The communities of the future will have directors of leisure time. The church of the future will have a minister of leisure time. The churches and the schools will face the phenomenal task of creating a new sense of purpose within people who will have more time available than they are prepared to use.

The Television Tube

The television tube has revolutionized life probably more than any other one factor. The average television set is turned on six hours a day in the average home. According to some mass media experts, sixty-five minutes each day are spent on commercials giving ninety separate pitches. 630 times a week, 32,000 times per year, the average person is bombarded by commercials in an unprecedented way. This means that through mass media a new art form has been produced which is molding the minds and wills of people. By the time a high school student reaches the day of graduation he has watched more than fifteen thousand hours of television and seen more than five hundred films at home or in the theater.

Marshall McLuhan, of Fordham University, one of the most controversial and provocative writers of this age, asserts that the new electronic mass media are shaping people as never before in history. He claims that the electronic influences are only deterministic if they are ignored. He pleads for an understanding of the youth who are growing up under this system and for all to get the best out of communications rather than the worst.

McLuhan's key thought is "The medium is the message." As English has been our form of mass medium, so now the film, through television and theater, has become our new language medium. Everyone must learn to develop habits of proper perception, analysis, and judgment in order to assimilate and utilize the input of the new language. Just as being literate is crucial for the proper communication of languages, being "cinemate" is now important to modern man.

The Christian community must become cinemate! It must learn to understand the new media and to utilize it. This means more than the development of preaching services and the televising of clergy-dominated panels. The new media demand new standards of excellence in the presentation of the Christian witness through all the art forms of television, radio, and theater.

One Roman Catholic archdiocese has developed a new closed-circuit TV system which is being made available to all faiths and denominations. The potential for real, vital life-changing, mind-shaping Christian education through this medium is fantastic. This approach alone will reshape the entire Christian education program of the modern church.

There is an openness today in the radio and television industry to what the church has to say to the world. What those in the industry suggest is that churchmen think and act as though the twenty-first century were truly here, with a positive affirmation of the message God has given to men. These channels of communication will open to a cinemate, committed people who will work according to the industry's standards of technological and cultural excellence.

The Strange New Church

The church in the twenty-first century will be a more authentic expression of Christian community than it was in the twentieth century. It will have risen above its preoccupation with buildings and programs and will find expression in new, radical forms of ministry. It will decentralize — resulting in more house churches in high-rise apartments, business offices, shopping centers, and central points of human contact like airports, superhighways, and cultural and leisure centers. The church institution and many of its buildings will still exist, but most of them will join together in clusters across denominational lines with a team ministry of specialists. One of the churches will function as a cathedral or hub of operation.

Fewer clergymen will be giving full time to the ministry, and a larger number of worker ministers (or priests) with theological training will work at secular jobs while giving part time to ministerial services.

The new breed of clergymen will be less concerned about dogma and doctrine and more vitally interested in the community and how to work through the implications of the gospel in that community. The image of a clean-shaven, black-suited, robed, white-shirted pastor will no longer exist.

Worship will be observed more commonly on weekdays, and new and more contemporary forms of music and language will be used. The choir will disappear from all but the large, affluent cathedral churches, and taped music will be substituted. Preaching through a closed-circuit TV arrangement with a central video station will be very common. The minister will give the bulk of his time to community involvement and to lay teaching in the academies and institutes which will emerge in metropolitan centers.

Some congregations will worship in their buildings only once a month, but on other Sundays families may gather around the TV set for Christian instruction and family devotions. The Sunday church school will be replaced by weekday Christian education institutes, organized as ecumenical institutions. Offerings for churches and religious endeavors will be made by credit card designations through one's local bank.

Much of what is now cumbersome church machinery will have disappeared, and the faithful Christian community will be freed to give time to meaningful evangelism in a world which will have become almost totally pagan. However, as a Christian minority on fire with the concern of the living risen Christ, a new Christian community will emerge with a style of life which will help bring reconciliation to a broken and bleeding world.

In the midst of such an emerging world the contemporary church is challenged to go beyond the walls which presently surround it.

❖❖❖ THE BATTLE
IN THE CHURCH

THE FUNERAL OF A CHURCH is a sad affair, where only a few tears are shed. On one such occasion a small group of people gathered in the large, drab, decaying building to hold their last service of worship. After 125 years in the midst of a teeming city which had dealt crushing blows to its dwindling membership, the tired, discouraged members had decided to give up and close the church's doors. But while these members mourned for their church and wondered about the future of other churches which were being affected by the deterioration of the inner city, a battle was raging in the ecclesiastical world. And that struggle continues!

The Opposing Forces

In the midst of the sweeping reformation which is shaking the very foundations of the contemporary Christian church, there is a life struggle going on between the two schools of

27

thought. The first school believes that the old, traditional forms of evangelism and churchmanship are adequate for the day and ought to be revived and renewed. The second opposing opinion is that the institutional church and all of the historic forms of evangelism and ministry related to it are no longer adequate for the times and ought to be buried. In between the opposing philosophies are the average church members, confused and baffled by the crossfire which they witness on the battlefield.

The traditionalists, who yearn for the "good old days" of their childhood when men were urged to accept Jesus as Savior through the influence of the little church on the corner and when there was a clear-cut distinction between the secular world and the religious world, are confused by the emphasis of men like Harvey Cox, who now seem to reverse the role of the religious and see Christians as the truly secular people in the world. They find it difficult to reconcile the role of Dr. Billy Graham, their "archbishop" and great hope for the world, with the action-oriented theology of a Dr. Cox or a Dr. Colin Williams.

On the other hand the experimentalists are those of every theological persuasion who believe that the institutional church is all finished as a force in history. They believe that money is being wasted on church buildings and programs and it would be better to do away with the traditional forms of church expression and move into the experimental ministries and paraparochial thrusts which can more adequately fulfill the purpose of God in the world. As with the traditionalists there are varying degrees of radicalism amongst the experimentalists. Some want to keep the traditional church institutions but bring changes in it after the fashion of Dr. Gordon Cosby of the Church of the Savior in Washington, D. C. The more extreme "young turks" in this movement would urge abandonment of all efforts to revive the dying church and encourage the redirection of energies and monies into a Christian penetration of the power structure of society. One such experiment is known as the "Metropolitan Associates of Philadelphia," whose purpose is to engage in action research for the church's ministry and participation in the modern metropolis with particular reference to the industrial, political, cultural, educational, and social sectors.[1] Recognizing that "the Bible knows no sharp distinction between the personal and the social, between the physical and the spiritual, between the secular and the sacred," [2] they urge the Christian church to lose its life as an institution and become the truly dynamic leaven of society discovering the God of history who is already in the world waiting to be joined in faithfulness by his children.

To be sure, it is difficult to describe briefly the two opposing factions in the church because there are no clear-cut distinctions between them. On the contrary, the very complex shades and differences among these elite battlers within the church contribute to the further bewilderment of the average church member. More people are to be found in the in-between land clinging to the best that is symbolized in the Christian church and its traditional approaches to the world. Yet they are open and seeking earnestly those new, radical forms which will make a more effective impact for Christ upon the urbanized society of this age.

These opposing factions can be brought together in this day when the Christian church stands at the very edge of its most glorious hour. While the great majority in the world couldn't care less about this struggle, those who love the church and who want to be faithful and obedient to God are searching for some way to heal the schism of the church and make a penetration of the world consistent with the will and purpose of Jesus Christ.

[1] Paul L. Stagg, *The Converted Church* (Valley Forge: The Judson Press, 1967), pp. 105-110.

[2] George D. Younger, *The Bible Calls for Action* (Valley Forge: The Judson Press, 1959), p. 20.

The beginning of understanding, for those who yearn to see the clear-cut answers to what is happening in the church today, is found in the discovery that the church is in the midst of one of the most earth-shaking reformations of its history. In his book *The Ferment in the Church*, Canon Roger Lloyd of Winchester Cathedral reminds us that this Reformation is very different from the old Reformation. The new Reformation does not offer the answers to the questions of the day, but catches us in a spirit of hesitancy and uncertainty.[3] Not only are the most sacrosanct institutions, like structures, forms, and customs, being called into question but the most taken-for-granted doctrines are being examined with a shockingly frank attitude of "honest to God" dimensions.

While they recognize that a reformation is underway, church members who sincerely desire renewal and change do not know where to turn. They hear the two symphonic pieces being played: one by the "return-to-the-good-old-days" orchestra and the other by the "forget-the-institutional-church-and-get-into-the-world" symphony. But because they seem to be opposing themes with resulting disharmony, the members block their ears or head for the exits.

Let's examine these two seemingly opposite themes.

A Mighty Army Falls

Whenever one holds up individual examples of success or failure, he runs the risk of making sweeping generalizations for the sake of supporting arguments. On the other hand, the old saying that "one picture is worth a thousand words" is still valid and a specific parish may reflect some of the problems in which the contemporary institutional church flounders. The parish church as we know it today grew out of the feudal system of our Western civilization. Life was centered in vil-

[3] Roger Lloyd, *The Ferment in the Church* (London: SCM Press Ltd., 1964; and New York: Morehouse-Barlow Co., Inc., 1964), p. 35.

lages, and the church of the village became the center and the regulator of Christian concepts and conduct. At the center of the residential groupings of life the village church of the feudal era helped to shape the minds of people through education, helped to shape the commercial life through the control of markets and guilds, helped to heal bodies through the practice of medicine, and helped to shape the value systems through the preaching of the gospel in terms of the life of that day. For almost a thousand years this has been the form and structure of the church — located at the heart of the residential community.

Then came the onslaught of urbanization. Beginning in the core cities, the residential church found itself in trouble as long ago as one to two hundred years. First in Europe and then later in the older cities of the eastern part of the United States, the inner-city churches began to find they were no longer residential churches. Their memberships had fled to suburbia, and during the last fifty years these churches have been disappearing.

Twenty-five years ago I became the pastor of such a church. Located in the inner city, my first church had fifty members, a congregation of fifteen, and a deteriorating building. At that time I was advised by more experienced ministers that two things would restore life to a dying church:

1. Devising a new methodology to reach the hostile, non-Anglo-Saxon, non-Protestant residents who lived within the vicinity of the church.

2. Preaching a gospel which helped men to know Christ and "to be born again."

While applying these principles with a moderate amount of success I wrote a B.D. thesis on the topic, "The Reconstruction of Churches in Deteriorated Areas." The model church, among many examples of inner-city institutions which were apparently adapting to the effects of urbanization, was the great Dudley Street Baptist Church of Roxbury, Massachusetts. This historic institution had at that time fifteen hundred members and boasted of baptisms every Sunday of the year. The church gave large amounts of money to the denominational mission program and engaged in many-faceted programs of Christian education and outreach to the community. Its ministers were always strong pulpiteers who attracted great crowds with their Bible preaching. But twenty-five years later that church, like so many others in similar situations, has virtually disappeared. The struggling congregation of seventy-five members lost its million dollar church plant to the urban renewal program of Boston because of the "under-utilization" of their facilities. Thus the members of the Dudley Street Baptist Church voted to merge with another struggling church of like size, and the final chapter on the "good old days" of Dudley Street has been closed.

What happened to this great church? There was a combination of many factors, but one of them stands out clearly. A *gospel of privatism* was preached in that church. Let no one misunderstand. The gospel of personal salvation does not necessarily have to be a gospel of privatism. The gospel of privatism has been concerned only about some people in a limited circle of society. In other words, many of the churches in the past sought a personal response from those who were the "nice people," or at least those whose culture and background were like that of the congregation. This is not to say that there was no concern for the poor or for the alcoholic who was causing a family breakup. But when the communities changed their complexion so that Italians, or Jews, or Poles, or Irish, or eventually Negroes were in the majority, then the privatistic gospel of churches could not reach out and attract such people.

Another devastating thing that happened to a church like Dudley Street was a failure to change the forms and structures of that church to meet the needs of the modern, secular city. Instead, such structures were defended and protected by the constituency as though they had been devised by the apostle Paul himself, rather than by the feudal system of the fifteenth century. Though the last pastor of that historic Roxbury church tried desperately to reform it and reshape its structures in order to reach out to the community, the old guard resisted his efforts and the church died. All the best preaching of the old-fashioned gospel could no longer save that historic church.

The White Flag of Experimentation

In church and religious circles all around the world, everyone hears and talks about the Church of the Savior in Washington, D. C. Stephen Rose in his book *The Grass Roots Church* describes this unique situation, noting that its pastor, Dr. Gordon Cosby, had advocated the complete overthrow of practically all present church structures.[4] Yet this church has distinguished itself as one of the dynamic, action-oriented, renewed congregations which has found new life through the acceptance of contemporary forms and the reshaping of its structures. Though the Church of the Savior has been held up as a model to churches in the United States, there are features about it that distinguish it from most activistic churches of the day. For example, a limited number of elite members are committed to a phenomenal level of participation through tithing, coffee-house activity, Bible study, and other forms of unique ministry. The average American parish, however, considers the Church of the Savior as a model too far above and removed from them to be of any practical help.

A real example of a reformed parish church which has accepted the principle of experimentation with the hope of finding spiritual renewal is the Woolwich parish of England where the Rev. Nicolas Stacey was rector. This church gained attention in Great Britain as one of the shining examples of experimental renewal. Yet in an article published in *The London*

---

[4] Stephen C. Rose, *The Grass Roots Church* (New York: Holt, Rinehart and Winston, Inc., 1966), p. 18.

Observer called "A Mission's Failure," Mr. Stacey asserted that he had led a dying, inactive church into a whirlwind of activity, and still renewal had not taken place.

The story of the renovation and restructuring of the Woolwich church is a thrilling one. The old Georgian building was completely remodeled making it contemporary and functional with an aesthetic beauty affecting all who enter it. A fully operating restaurant was created for working people, and a unique discotheque was started for the youth of the community. One of the sealed-off balconies was made into an attractive drop-in lounge for those who sought rest and quiet in the midst of a busy working day. Thus the church building, functionally redesigned, with its doors open fifteen hours a day, was being used by an average of fifteen hundred people a week who entered it for the purpose of playing, eating, resting, counseling, praying, and worshiping.

Under the leadership of the Reverend Mr. Stacey and with the encouragement and counsel of Bishop John Robinson, a new, strong team of gifted priests, each with expertise in some special area of community life, was formed. They launched out enthusiastically upon a community-related ministry which involved not only them but their church. The Woolwich parish team ministry and reformed church gained the attention of the secular world. But in a personal interview Mr. Stacey reported that, although he and his team had touched the lives of two thousand couples or families over a period of ten years, he could point to only one couple where any meaningful transformation of life in terms of Christian values and concerns had taken place! In spite of the fact that this team had had relationships with thousands through baptisms, burials, marriages, counseling situations, and programs of the Woolwich church, its leader felt that all this activism and experimentation had been almost useless.

These two cited examples of churches attempting to meet the current age through the preaching of privatism or through the gospel of activism demonstrate why today's members of the Christian church are baffled and discouraged as they face technopolis. They ask, "If preaching the old-fashioned gospel is not adequate and if reforming the present structures does not renew, then what's the use?" Unfortunately all are seeking simple answers to complex questions. Clearly, two assumptions are held in common by the two cited churches. The first is that both churches assume that the clergy-centered approach to the residential area is still the way to minister to society, and the second is that the residential parish system of the past age can still be developed. Both of these are false assumptions which can no longer weather the storm of urbanization.

We must not forget that for centuries we have thought of the clergyman as being the man at the center of all things; this situation is no longer true, and the church must face the fact.

Churches of today still talk about the "family church" for all families as though the church can adequately minister through family structures. This, too, is no longer possible in a day when families are fragmented into various worlds. Churches forget that father goes off to spend his time in his business world, while mother may also be in her working world, and the children spend the major part of their time in the world of education. Then each of these family members separate daily to enter their separate worlds of leisure.

The modern church still finds it difficult to believe that each of these separate worlds has a different language, a unique set of values, its own group relationships, and a special kind of secularism (or god) which has not been penetrated or influenced by the gospel of privatism or by the cleverness of radical churchmanship.

Because secularism dominates these worlds, the tendency of some Christians is to withdraw and form into pious cliques for the sake of spiritual preservation. Still others decide that the only way is to throw in their lot and lose all special identification as the "peculiar" people.

A Lesson from History

History teaches us great lessons about the church's failure to come to grips with the new worlds which have grown out of the old worlds. One of the most important of these lessons comes out of the context of Germany and the era of Hitler.

My wife and I were reminded of this while walking the streets of Amsterdam, Holland. In searching for the Anne Frank Huis on Prinzgracht Street we made inquiry of a Dutch gentleman as to the whereabouts of the house. He pointed to a church spire and said, "See that — it's right behind that church; that's Old West."

It was just a house among houses, squeezed in between rows of typical Dutch dwellings. I pulled the brass knob on the door, and a young university student ushered us up the steep stairs. We were shown the small factory on the first floor which functioned while the Franks hid silently above. Then the secret bookcase-door swung open, and we climbed up a still steeper stairway into the bedroom of Mr. and Mrs. Frank and one of their children. It was exactly as it had been left the day the Nazi troopers came to take them off to the concentration camp — emptying the room except for scattered papers on the floor. It was among these papers that Anne Frank's personal diary was found.

The next room was Anne's. On the walls were the pasted pictures of Deanna Durbin, and other pictures clipped from newspapers. While the university student was explaining that this room was exactly as left by Anne, I stood by the open window overlooking the city. The same white lace curtains, now tattered and yellow, hung there. I peeked through them, and there breaking the skyline of Amsterdam was the Old West Church. This was the church that rang its clear-tinkling bells (so typical of Dutch churches) announcing the hours of the long fear-filled days and nights when the Jews hid from the Nazis.

In looking at the church spire I thought of one of the entries that Anne had made in her diary. On that day the Franks had heard about a decree which had been sent out through Amsterdam. The Jews were to shop only during certain limited hours in the day; they were not permitted to ride on public transportation; and among many more regulations they *were not to be caught talking with Christians at any time — anywhere!*

What thoughts did Anne have of the church which spawned such warped minds? Did she think about their being called "Christians"? Did she contemplate the fact that the Christ they claimed to follow was a Jew who taught love for all? Did she wonder about the hymn singers and Scripture readers who claimed to be a superior race? How did she keep her balance of mind in thinking of the evil of those who claimed to be good? And yet, she, who did not profess to be a follower of the Savior of Galilee, wrote: ". . . in spite of everything I still believe that people are really good at heart." [5]

Today this little bedroom of Amsterdam becomes a prayer room for all Christians who call ourselves the believers in the Christ. But it also becomes a modern wailing wall for those who would weep over the institutional church, admitting its failures and praying for its mission.

Has the church learned its lesson? There are those today in Europe who think not. I talked with one university graduate student from Bonn who believes Naziism is slowly being revived in Germany. A Dutch Jew, whose four brothers and two sisters were exterminated at Dachau, was returning on a train from Dachau after having made a memorial pilgrimage to this place which sickens one beyond words. He shared with me his feeling that anti-semitism was very much alive in Germany. He had spent several days in fun-loving Munich and felt the hatred once again held by the German people there.

Yet Munich has 163 churches, of which 130 are Roman

[5] Anne Frank, *The Diary of a Young Girl* (New York: Doubleday & Company, Inc., 1952), p. 229.

Catholic, and it is the headquarters of the Lutheran church. Is the church still so tied up in its administrative duties that it fails to believe that the horror-filled days of Hitler can return?

While we are asking this question of the German church, I am reminded of talking with a German pastor in Mainz, who, after being queried about the revival of anti-semitism asked, "Is anti-semitism dead in the United States? And what of your Christian people's attitudes toward the Negro?"

Standing in the window of Anne Frank's room, my mind went back to the rainy afternoon when I arrived alone and weary in Selma, Alabama. Riding on the bus from Montgomery to Selma, I passed a church which had a banner draped on its front announcing that there was a state-wide youth rally going on and the theme was "Christian Witness." The white, chorus-singing youth seemed to be totally unaware of the relationship between their theology and the little band of blacks who stood in the mud some blocks away, looking into the faces of the grim state police who surrounded them with patrol cars and lengths of rope.

There is very little that separates Amsterdam and Berlin from Alabama and Boston. The basic attitudes of people are the same — people who have become so numbed by the institutionalism of the church that the dynamic theology of life-giving love in the flesh has become a remote reality. Precisely at this point of bifurcation of life and theology the traditionalists and the experimentalists find themselves in need of a common repentance experience. We have all encouraged piety apart from public responsibility as well as activity apart from personal Christ-motivated commitment. Canon Roger Lloyd put it in still another way:

> If the reformation is to be creative, it is therefore most important to marry together the two words Traditionalist and Innovator and to see them both as partners in the fellowship of the Kingdom. For that is

what they are. Each has something essential to give to the growth of the Kingdom of God. Neither can give it in isolation, but only in fellowship with the other. If the traditionalist is tempted to live in the past, it is bad. If the innovator tends to live in the future, it is far worse. For this is to make the present pay for the future and the price of the future is higher by far than the price of the past. But past and future join hands in the present and traditionalist and innovator are together servants of the timeless now, and those who are alive in it. It is the chain of timelessness within time that saves both, and the rest of us with them. We are all part of history and history is now.[6]

The Christian church is facing the most glorious hour in its history. The forces within the church must become united like rivulets of water descending from the mountain heights, uniting as a mighty rushing force, bringing life and renewal to the parched people of the earth.

[6] Lloyd, *op. cit.*, pp. 49-50.

❖❖❖ THE RECONCILING
COMMUNITY REDISCOVERED

IN AN AGE WHEN CHRISTIANS are told they live in a secular society but ought not to be afraid of this because God has created the secular city as his instrument of redemption, they are still confused over the question of how to be "in the world" but "not of the world." After generations of teaching about the dangers of worldliness of the secular, now the average layman is perplexed by the call to a new kind of "holy worldliness" as propounded by Dietrich Bonhoeffer and others. He instinctively responds to this call for "holy worldliness" but has had little biblical or theological training to prepare him for what it implies.

The Rebirth of an Old Idea

We have been made aware of the destructive aspects of the bifurcation of the church's place in the world. The way Adolf Hitler used this to manipulate the church in Germany to a position of apathy and impotence while he exterminated the Jews and launched military attacks upon weaker neighbors is well known; but what is not well known is the emergence at the same time of a renewed, revitalized, dynamic minority of Christians led by such figures as Dietrich Bonhoeffer, Eberhard Mueller, and Horst Symanowski. Bonhoeffer gave his life in a Nazi concentration camp, and his posthumously published works have had a revolutionary effect upon the Christian church. Eberhard Mueller founded the German Evangelical Lay Academy movement and has done more to bring about dialogue between the Christian minority of Germany and the business and professional world than any other man of the century. Horst Symanowski has pioneered in discovering ways to penetrate the industrial sector of society and made real again the presence of the Christian community among smokestacks and noisy machines. The Reformed Church of Germany has taught us a way to rise above the privatistic gospel approach. It also shows us that merely contemporizing the old institutional church by jazzing up its worship or modernizing its facilities is not enough.

It is important to note that these men did not abandon the Christian church when they sought a means to bring renewal to it. They did, however, make the decision to lose their lives in the world and move out into a painful and promising relationship which would bring about transformation and reconciliation. Men like Dr. Mueller and Horst Symanowski gathered small dedicated groups of Christians around them and proceeded to become the "salty Christians" that Hans-Ruedi Weber writes about.

Thus, an idea as old as the church itself was reborn: the creation of the cell which evangelized society from within. Douglas Webster in *Yes to Mission* reminds us that we can speak of success or failure in mission only in terms of witness and obedience, not results. In deploring the concept of mission dependence upon foreign missionaries, he quotes Adrian

Hastings, a Roman Catholic missionary scholar from Uganda who says, "The foreign missionary's job is to create a cell which will then evangelize society from within." [1] What the church has forgotten is the constant and perpetual need for the creation of such cells in *every area where the church exists!*

Lyle Schaller, Regional Church Planning Director for Northeastern Ohio, writes:

> Two other changes will influence the ministry of tomorrow's church. One is the already growing recognition that in many situations the pastor cannot function effectively in the isolation which is so typical of today's church. One answer to the problems of isolation is the group ministry. . . . [The other is:] *The remaining minority may resurrect the New Testament concept of the church as a gathered community bound together by a spiritual, economic, and vocational discipline.* [2]

In *The Church Inside Out* Professor J. C. Hoekendijk, of Holland, tries to force us to see the position in which Christianity will find itself in the not too distant future. The population explosion has already moved the church into more and more of a minority position. The church must accept the fact of the passing of "multitudinism." The erosion of church life and the breaking up of local congregations is creating new cells, nuclei, and teams. The church of tomorrow will find itself "in a *diaspora* situation: living in dispersion as thinly spread minority groups. Toynbee advises us therefore — as a mental training for what is to come — to study the Jewish diaspora again seriously." [3] In short we must hear the call to become a *dedicated minority!*

We do not need to wait for a diaspora or for the institutional church to become the small cell within the remnants of

[1] Douglas Webster, *Yes to Mission* (New York: The Seabury Press, Inc., 1966), p. 36. © SCM Press Ltd., 1966.

[2] Lyle E. Schaller, *Planning for Protestantism in Urban America* (Nashville: Abingdon Press, 1965), pp. 202-203 (italics ours).

[3] J. C. Hoekendijk, *The Church Inside Out* (London: SCM Press Ltd., 1964; and Philadelphia: The Westminster Press, 1966), p. 181. (See Arnold Toynbee, "The Diaspora Age," *Issues,* September, 1960.)

a dying Christendom. We already have the cells and units for renewed life within every existing local congregation! Every pastor is aware of this and suffers great anguish when this potential manpower is manipulated into wasting energies on the housekeeping chores of the average institutional church.

About 5 to 10 percent of the committed and dedicated members of any congregation carry the main responsibilities of that church, moving out beyond the usual, ordinary, commonplace members to places of leadership. Why not recognize that the local church is a "split-level" community and seek ways to free that "cell" of the dedicated minority for dispersion into the world in a meaningful way? The Christian church of today should be attentive to Stephen Rose when he says:

> Certainly the idea of a dedicated minority is not new and, in the past, it has functioned well as an approach to change. It is at present the most likely pattern for a renewal movement among the American Protestant churches.[4]

Though Mr. Rose may have in mind the formation of such groups outside the church, a case can be made for seeking out those people in local congregations who are eager to enter into a relationship with Christ and his world — but are not being encouraged or guided in this direction! It is such people, concerned and committed, who should be unshackled by the church of today so that they may give their time and energies to the renewal of the world through the mission of the church.

Members of the church need to take a new look at the world in which they live. The idea of community is now central in our pluralistic life. The very fragmentation of society into various worlds of family, business, education, politics, and leisure has forced the emergence of the larger community. Community has become the foundation upon which these worlds relate to each other and thus find meaning for life.

[4] Rose, *op. cit.*, p. 23.

Originally, the church was a "cell" or "community" within the simple community. They gathered around Christ, learned from him, and became the salt or the light of the world. Eventually the gathered Christians became the center of the community; and in the simple, rural atmosphere of the eighth to the tenth centuries all of life was affected by their witness.

With the coming of the age of technology and the splitting of this centralized, simple world, the growth of great cities changed the community into a complex, sprawling monstrosity. The local parish no longer influenced the community through its control of families. The individual found himself pulled away from the close relationship he once had with the church and with his simple world. Then began the breakdown between the community and the church.

Many refuse to see this breakdown and accept it for what it is because they are removed from the inner city where this situation is most manifest. The great urban centers of America have been increasingly abandoned by those who continue to hide their heads in the sands of suburbia and small-town America. But the remnants still struggling on the firing lines of the core-cities understand the need for community in this century. They see it in urban renewal, in community agencies, in public housing, in metropolitan transportation, and in other such forms. The residents, hidden in the milieu of urbanization, struggle to find their own sense of community through common bonds of identification and service.

The time has come for the institutional church to accept the fact of the church's removal from the center of community and discover new ways to move back into the worlds of family life, business operation, education, politics, and leisure. A small, dedicated minority of disciplined Christians from each local church can become "the reconciling community" within the larger community. This is the original reason for the church's existence. As the leaven in the world, the reconciling community penetrates and changes the community around it.

Looking at the Bible

The story of the children of Israel is one of a community dispersed throughout the world as the reconciling community. We read with new interest the following Old Testament passages:

Thou hast made us like sheep for slaughter,
    and hast scattered us among the nations.
Thou hast sold thy people for a trifle,
    demanding no high price for them.

Thou hast made us the taunt of our neighbors,
    the derision and scorn of those about us.
Thou hast made us a byword among the nations,
    a laughingstock among the peoples.
                                (Psalm 44:11-14)

I have given you as a covenant to the people,
    a light to the nations,
    to open the eyes that are blind,
to bring out the prisoners from the dungeon,
    from the prison those who sit in darkness.
                                (Isaiah 42:6-7)

"You are my witnesses," says the Lord,
    "and my servant whom I have chosen,
that you may know and believe me
    and understand that I am He.
Before me no god was formed,
    nor shall there be any after me.
I, I am the Lord,
    and besides me there is no savior.
I declared and saved and proclaimed,
    when there was no strange god among you;
    and you are my witnesses," says the Lord.
                                (Isaiah 43:10-12)

Remember these things, O Jacob,
    and Israel, for you are my servant;
I formed you, you are my servant;

O Israel, you will not be forgotten by me.
I have swept away your transgressions like a cloud,
    and your sins like a mist;
return to me, for I have redeemed you.
(Isaiah 44:21-22)

In the New Testament we read in the Gospels that Jesus sent the disciples into the communities of Palestine with specific instructions to become the reconciling community with a unique ministry to those in need:

> And remain in the same house, eating and drinking what they provide, for the laborer deserves his wages; do not go from house to house. Whenever you enter a town and they receive you, eat what is set before you; heal the sick in it and say to them, "The kingdom of God has come near to you" (Luke 10:7-9).

In the same chapter of the Gospel of Luke is the story of the good Samaritan who, motivated by human compassion and divine concern, stopped in the middle of a busy day to bind up the wounds of the beaten man on the road. Members of the reconciling community are not just do-gooders, they are channels of God's compassion and love. They are the partakers of Christ's suffering and the sharers of man's pain. This is why our Lord chose a common symbol of community, the breaking of bread around a table, as the vehicle to aid the members of the community to recall the central fact of love and suffering.

The early church, compelled by the presence of the living Christ, gathered itself as the reconciling community bound up in common concerns and characteristics. Luke tells us in Acts "they were all together in one place." Later he also informs us of their communal living in which they shared property and goods. They articulated with boldness a new style of life which created a condition that "turned the world upside down."

The apostle Paul in writing to the Corinthians said: "For

just as the body is one and has many members, and all the members of the body, though many, are one body, so it is with Christ" (1 Corinthians 12:12).

The commentator in *The Interpreter's Bible* makes the following observation about this passage:

The implication is clear, and it underlines the apostle's writings, that the church exists to continue the propagation of the gospel to the whole world; that since it is animated by the spirit and life, the knowledge and wisdom, which find their source in its great "head," it is his continued incarnation in the world. Its supreme function is to perpetuate and spread his spirit everywhere, until the whole of life becomes a like organism, illumined, inspired, controlled, and dominated by the Lord of all good life. The process is to go on until the sovereignty of the world passes into the sovereignty of God and his Christ; until, in effect, the whole world of humanity in all its aspects becomes a church. For this great conception of their significance in the life of the world, and of their part in the unfolding of the great purposes of God, *the apostle is constantly preparing the Christian communities with which he has to deal and which he loves so dearly.*[5]

The reason for the reconciling community's existence is articulated in 1 Corinthians 14:1 by Paul: "Make love your aim." *This is the crux and scope of Christian evangelism,* but it is not ordinary, human love; it is what Paul was speaking of when he wrote, "If I give away all I have, and if I deliver my body to be burned, but have not love . . ." *(agape),* the unique Christ-centered love which puts a man in touch with God.

Bonhoeffer in *Life Together* states the idea this way:

Christianity means community through Jesus Christ and in Jesus Christ. No Christian community is more or less than this. Whether it be a brief, single encounter or the daily fellowship of years, Christian community is only this. We belong to one another only through and in Jesus Christ.

What does this mean? It means, first, that a Christian needs others because of Jesus Christ. It means, second, that a Christian comes to

[5] John Short, *The Interpreter's Bible* (Nashville, Abingdon Press, 1953), Vol. 10, p. 158 (italics ours).

others only through Jesus Christ. It means, third, that in Jesus Christ we have been chosen from eternity, accepted in time, and united for eternity.[6]

The Christian community is that unique gathering of people who have been drawn together for the purpose of changing the wider community and the people within it. In the Christian community is generated that love-force in people which becomes more powerful through small action groups. The Christian community is the bringing together of those who believe the presence of Jesus Christ can be made effective and real in individuals and in society.

New Beginnings for a Divided Church

In terms of the thesis stated earlier in this book that there is a battle going on within the Christian church between the traditionalists and the experimentalists, unity between these factions will be found only in the reconciling community concept. Beginning with the acceptance of servanthood in Jesus Christ, the contemporary Christian must admit that it is not a question of following one extreme or the other but of understanding the present world and discovering ways to communicate the truth of God to that world.

The local parish is still the place where the reconciling community can be found and nurtured. To get started, all any key member of a church has to do is to invite a dozen interested people into his home and suggest that they might take upon themselves common disciplines of spiritual nourishment and community involvement. To be sure, some pastors hearing of this might think a subversive element is forming in the church, but others will fall upon their knees in thanksgiving to God!

In some cases a pastor will have to take the initiative and suggest to a few key people that they drop out of the usual

[6] Dietrich Bonhoeffer, *Life Together*, John W. Doberstein, trans. (New York: Harper & Row, Publishers, 1954; and London: SCM Press Ltd., 1965), p. 21.

"churchy chores" and become a specialized task force meeting for prayer, instruction, and eventual involvement.

There will be risks in fostering the reconciling community within any local church. The people in the smaller group will be tempted to become a piously exclusive set; they may even find such a joy in this involvement that they will become impatient with the "ninety and nine of the fold" and dissociate themselves from the rest of the congregation. But such risks must be taken with complete trust in the Holy Spirit.

One thing can happen: The reconciling community can blend the traditional expressions of the church with the experimental innovations and, in a sense, become to the church what a research division is to an industry.

A major difficulty in suggesting that a group of people be set aside for a radically new and different kind of relationship within the church, and outside in the world, is in not having many examples of what can be done. However, some significant communities have been formed which may give some hints to those who desire to start some attempts in this direction.

Models to Look At

The Iona Community founded in 1938 by Dr. George MacLeod (now Lord MacLeod) has served as a model for inspiration to the church of Christ. It came into being when Dr. MacLeod was minister of the Govan Old Parish Church in Glasgow, Scotland. He arrived at the conclusion that some new form of Christian community should be formed in order to find new ways of witness in the midst of an industrial society.

With six young ministers and six young craftsmen he went to the Isle of Iona to rebuild the ruined Abbey there, not merely because of the need of rebuilding it but as a way to bring a small disciplined group together in a common life of work and worship. Out of this common sharing of muscle and prayer the small group was to return to the mainland ready for the encounter with urban society.

Those who become members of the Iona Community do not merely retreat from life for a period of time during the summer, but rather pledge themselves, as a small group of only 150 members, to a more meaningful expression of Christian living through efforts:

1. to find new patterns for the life of the church so that it may make an effective witness;

2. to find for themselves in their jobs in industry, education, or other fields the full contribution which they can make as Christians to the life of the world;

3. to find how they may fulfill their commitment to peace-making in their congregations, in their jobs, and in their political and social life.

Though the Iona Community is well known throughout the world, very few outside of Scotland know of the existence of Iona's Community House in Glasgow. Yet the Iona spirit as manifested in and through the Community House shows more fully what could happen in a local church which covenants to bring about the reconciling community within its structure.

The Reverend Douglas Alexander, Warden of the Community House, in the center of the core-city of Glasgow, shared with me the history of the place, which was first a lavish mansion, then a warehouse, and finally a series of industrial workshops. As a laboratory for living-out and working-out a Christian style of life, he showed me how it is meeting many great needs in the heart of Glasgow.

The Community House has three simple reasons for being. It is a center for meeting, a center for study and training, and a center for worship. It sounds like any ordinary church, doesn't it? The difference is found in the way in which these are related to each other and to the community. For example, a restaurant there with a permanent staff of seventeen full-time workers and twenty-five volunteers serves over 700 each day.

It is on the street level where people from every walk of life feel free to enter. A city bus terminal is located across the street from the Community House, and passengers, drivers, and conductors all frequent the restaurant.

As one steps into the restaurant, he sees at its center, toward the back of the large room, a chapel with lighted candles and cross. Each day of the week at noontime a brief service of worship is held. No one is compelled to attend it, but neither can he escape its meaning — that God is present in the ordinary places of life and that the people serving in the restaurant are part of a community which cares for the rest of the community!

The only way to participate in any of the events of the House's program (seminar, consultation, social workers' club, engineers' forum, or alcoholics anonymous and gamblers anonymous) is to enter through the restaurant area with its tables, chairs, and dishes, where ordinary people sit around and one is reminded of God's presence among his people. Neither can they avoid the open chapel which reminds one of the relationship between the Creator and his creatures! This is the blending of the experimental with the traditional in community expression!

Another community, perhaps little known outside of England, is the Mayflower Community established by the Reverend David Sheppard some ten years ago. A dying Anglican church was taken over by this dynamic young priest, who had formerly been a national cricket hero for the British sports fans. He gathered about himself a team of twenty people from every walk of life who live together as a community on the property where the church is located. They are in the midst of East London "flats" which house 65,000 people who work at the docks and shipyards.

David Sheppard informed me that the main target of this church and Christian community is "the happy pagan." This is the person who is perfectly content with life as it is — making a living, enjoying ordinary comforts, and seeking the maximum of earthly pleasures.

The Mayflower Community has made an impact upon the area. One man named George, whose life was transformed because of the Community, joined the group and became its youth leader. He died recently and has been greatly missed. David Sheppard said of him, "They all loved George because he was so earthy." Perhaps he was saying that the Christian community can have its effect only to the degree that its members remember, "there I go, but for the grace of God."

The Mayflower Community is strongly evangelical. It establishes small units for Bible study and prayer in the flats. It prints its own material for education and evangelism. It confronts persons with the need to make a decision about the place of their life in relation to God and his plan. Though it makes no great claims of success or even parish renewal, a significant group of families from the flats have discovered a new direction for themselves and their children.

Located not far from the Mayflower Community in London is another significant experiment being carried on by a young Anglican priest from New Zealand. The Reverend Michael Elliott arrived in England, after study under Harvey Cox in Boston, seeking an opportunity for involvement in the inner city. He was located in St. Christopher's parish in the "Elephant and the Castle" area of London.

This church, like many around it, had been in trouble for years. It had been without a parish priest for two years because no clergyman wanted his family to live in such an undesirable area. A typical Sunday congregation was composed of twenty from this cockney district. There were four other Anglican churches near it, all of them in the same dire circumstances.

Associated with St. Christopher's Church is an adjoining building which was called Pembroke House and formerly served as a social center for the area. Taking advantage of the

Pembroke House, which had sleeping rooms in it, Mr. Elliott began to gather about himself people with a concern for becoming part of a team interested in human needs. Not all members in this group even claimed to be Christian; yet one who was a professed agnostic manifested a most Christlike spirit and started a club for the deaf!

One of the unique aspects of this community was the "open door policy" which existed for the cockney youths from the streets. The group living at Pembroke House ate in a common dining room at the street level. The main door of the house was opened at 2:00 P.M. daily, when young men and women were permitted the freedom of entering, sitting at the table, visiting a special cookie jar, chatting with Vicar Elliott, or playing games in the game room. On Sunday many of these same young people were in the worship service although only one out of eighty British people attend church services on an average Sunday.

Believing in Bonhoeffer's suggestion concerning a religious community of radically secular people who may be from various professional levels of life, Michael Elliott is reaching into a community where boys and girls know dope at its worst, have already established police records, and believe that "everyone's trying to do me in."

These three communities are cited as models, among others like the Taize Community of France, the Koinonia Community of Georgia, and the Ecumenical Institute of Chicago, because they each offer possibilities which may be incorporated into the local parish. The Iona Community seeks, out of the inspiration of retreat and worship, to penetrate the world as a disciplined band of disciples pledged to a common philosophy of mission. The Mayflower Community, as a gathered group of dedicated evangelicals living in the midst of a world of happy pagans, seeks to identify with them through a living relationship of counseling, visitation, community programs, and involvement. The Pembroke Community, made up of Christians and non-Christians who earn their living in the secular world during the day and who relate to the people among whom they live as a family that cares, is teaching that being human among those who are being dehumanized is also an aspect of Christian responsibility.

Perhaps, from the example of one of these communities, some small group of caring members of a local church will be led to launch out as a renewed community within God's world.

❖❖❖ MARKS OF THE
RECONCILING COMMUNITY

"WHAT MAKES THE CHRISTIAN CHURCH any different from any other organizations in the world?" asked a caustic, bitter young man who was participating in a panel on, "The Church in the World." He went on to affirm his belief that there was nothing distinct, unique, or challenging in the contemporary church. While this may be true in all too many cases, it is not as true in others. But the larger question is: How can Christians who do want to be different be helped to find a more meaningful expression of their faith? They must have ministerial leadership and encouragement, but they must also find ways to unite themselves with those who are seeking ways to become the servant people.

Here is a simple plan. One or two people can take the initiative to discover five to ten people within the church who would be willing to gather in a home and discuss the possibility of forming a community cell which would seek to develop its own style of study, worship, and action. This group would come to grips with ideas of incarnational presence, organizational reformation, and the articulation of Christian disciplines and beliefs. In other words the group would determine to manifest the marks of the reconciling community. In attempting to recover the idea of the inner community of shock troops within the institutional church it is natural to seek some identifiable marks which can serve as goals toward becoming that kind of servant people. Let's think about these marks.

The Person Is at the Center

Because we live in a time of quantitative thinking, we naturally act as organizational man and too often forget the existence of *people as individual persons.*

The mission strength of the Christian church has always depended upon the person who was gripped inwardly by the presence of Christ and turned outward with compassion toward others. Granted, too many Christians have seen potential converts as "souls to be won" and no more, but those who have seen the needs of the whole person have often kindled a fire within others which resulted in a new faith and a new life.

Only twelve men who responded to the call of "follow me" started the great sweep of history in the name of a Person crucified upon a cross. Since that time other individuals have felt the presence of Jesus Christ and identified with their neighbor, with a cause or a movement, with an agency or an institution, with a system or a structure, to become Christ's agents of reconciliation.

The old English word "parson," meaning "person," identified the one who lived among the people and related to the systems of a simplistic society. But the parson was moved aside by urbanization and the development of a pluralistic society; and the "person" who lived among them sharing the problems of work and play, life and death, became the pastor, vicar, minister, or rector, the man to hear on Sunday, to visit during the time of crisis, or to consult for the special events of life!

Because ministers and priests have realized this setting aside and have been frustrated by it, the "worker-priest" movement has arisen in an attempt to replace the professional clergyman with the "person." However, this movement still limits the Christian community by including only a specialized, professional type of Christian elite.

What is needed today alongside of the "worker-priest" movement is a *"lay-priest"* movement. The "person" of the reconciling community must be the *layman!*

In the Gospel of John we read in the prologue: "In the beginning was the Word, and the Word was with God, and the Word was God. . . . In him was life, and the life was the light of men." This is the description of the coming of Jesus as God's Word — God's communication with men! Then John wrote: "There was a man sent from God, whose name was John. . . . He was not the light, but came to bear witness to the light." God came in the flesh, through Christ, in order that the people might know what God was like. "He who has seen me has seen the Father." The person of God was known through the person of Christ. But a man named John was also sent from God to be the "person" to point to that Person.

The coming of God in the flesh we call the incarnation, but was the incarnation a single event in history which soon passed? Or does God still send men like John to point the way, to be the persons through whom the living Christ now speaks, moves, and changes?

Some Christians ask why some people think that involvement in the racial struggle, in problems relating to inner-city housing, or affiliation with community organizations, is a form of Christian evangelism; the answer is that faithful followers of Christ believe in the presence of the Person. The living Christ, through the members of the Christian community who bear his burden and share his love, is himself present as the Person. A member of the Christian community knows that his presence at the side of the needy, dispossessed, angry, unloved, bewildered, or even the happy pagan, makes real the presence of Christ. We would agree with those theologians who tell us that Christ is present in his world without us, but we would add that the presence of Christ is more real where flesh and blood, tears and sweat, smiles and hands are offered to members of the larger community. Thus involvement in social problems is not social action for action's sake, or humane concern prompted by human motivation, but rather it is Incarnational Evangelism. The person who knows that Christ speaks through human flesh, revealing God's love and concern for others, making Christ real to them.

The validity of this kind of evangelism is demonstrated by the response of one woman who lived in an area served by a Christian center.

When one of the workers at the center moved away she said, "When I met these people of the center, I never believed that there was anything left of charity and love, but this man talked with us and shared our problems for two years! I know a new way of life now. I've got six children and I want to live in this neighborhood and get along. Some people think we are bums. We are poor but we are also human — but this man cared — and he made the difference!"

When the British Broadcasting Company visited Michael Elliott at the Pembroke Community House in London to make a television special on his work in the inner city, the director of the program asked Mr. Elliott what he was doing that some other social agency couldn't do just as well. It was not easy to answer such a provocative question, but the person who becomes the channel of the presence of the Person of Christ is different! He meets the needs of the whole person; and that's what salvation is all about!

So, the members of the reconciling community covenant to

become the presence, the person, the parson alongside of a neighbor, within a movement, or as part of a power structure. Accepting this kind of action as a valid form of evangelism helps to eliminate the friction and separation between those who believe in saving souls and those who urge the penetration of power structures. It is not a question of either-or, but both-and!

At a recent conference on home missions the question was raised about how becoming involved in community organizations, or social welfare agencies, or low-income housing, could possibly be viewed as any more than social action for action's sake. Where did evangelism fit into this kind of contemporary involvement? The answer is in the idea of incarnational presence; the person there becomes the living person of Christ in the flesh.

Responsiveness to the Living Presence of Christ

The encounter of the living risen Christ with his disciples set their hearts aglow with a desire to gather together for instruction and mutual strengthening in order to be the reconciling community within the world. There was a time in history, a moment of decision, when each of the disciples settled for himself the question of who Jesus Christ really was and by what right he demanded allegiance. This has been true of his followers through all the ensuing years. They have known his resurrection in their own experience and believed him to truly be "the man for others." Consequently, in faith they have placed themselves in his hands. If there are those who think this sounds like revivalism and a restoration of the altar call, then let it be so. The difference between this and revivalism is in accepting the fact that there is no single form of response to Christ which is more valid than any other. Each local church must work out an expression of Christian decision appropriate to its own cultural background and meaningful to its membership. What is central in answering the call of

Christ in a tangible way which reveals the marks of his presence and results in a community of action?

> The servant Church is not simply serving men on their terms; it serves God by ministering in judgment and promise within the structures of man's world. The laity is, thus, the prophetic fellowship which summons men to reflection upon their responsibility for shaping the future. This prophetic fellowship has no special program or political party; it has only the commitment to the New Mankind which God has created in his Son, the mankind of love and reconciliation which discloses the true being of all men and their life together. In the name of this future to which all men belong and which is theirs to acknowledge, the prophetic fellowship summons men and women in every walk of life to consider this gift as disclosing their true identity and ultimate hope.[1]

The response of youth, and often adults in the prime of their lives, to the challenge of the Peace Corps and Vista programs ought to demonstrate the church's failure to present the full, hard, life-demanding claims of Christ upon his followers. Much of the rationalization for caution about raising emotions in appealing to people for a decision for total commitment has been the result of the refusal of the church to confront a touchy issue. When a member of the Church of the Savior in Washington, D.C. was asked why he had left another church in the capital city to join the Church of the Savior, he responded by saying, "When I went to other churches they gave me something to do. When I went to the Church of the Savior they asked me for my life."

Every young minister of the gospel should be required to serve on a foreign mission field. He will discover, in the newer fields particularly, this responsiveness to the demands of Christ. The one great impact made upon me when I served in Mexico for several years as a missionary was the willingness of people to respond literally to the call: "He who does not take his cross and follow me is not worthy of me. He who finds his life

[1] Gibson Winter, *The New Creation as Metropolis* (New York: The Macmillan Company, 1963), p. 72.

will lose it, and he who loses his life for my sake will find it"
(Matthew 10:38, 39).

Flexible Organizational Structure

The church is being led today by clergymen who have been
trapped in the torturing snare of rigid institutionalism. These
ministers and priests do not stand alone, however. They have
a dedicated core of people who, likewise, do not know how to
break the calcifying, immobilizing structures which have become the contemporary church. We all recognize that these
structures developed as the church took on the folkways and
culture of its times. Now, what can be done about it? How
can we break loose and move forward?

The answer depends upon that small group of people who
will to become the reconciling community within the church.
They may have to be content to remain a secret cell waiting
patiently for the right moment to act, or they may devise a
plan or strategy to upset the church fathers and bring about
a structural reformation. Whatever takes place, they will inevitably organize! But history warns us that even significant
movements within rigid structures eventually develop harden-
ing of the arteries and themselves need reformation. It is important to recognize this danger from the start and build-in a
flexibility which will make it possible for any church movement to change or even to die.

The text of a keynote speech given before a Joint Urban
Strategy Conference in St. Louis during the summer of 1967
appeared in *Church in Metropolis.*[2] This address was given by
Jake McCarthy, a Roman Catholic layman and member of the
Teamsters Joint Council of St. Louis. He made a strong plea
for the church to shift over from institution to movement. Mr.
McCarthy said:

[2] Jake McCarthy, "From Institution to Movement," *Church in Metropolis* (Summer Issue, 1967), pp. 3-4. Copyright 1968 by Joint Strategy
and Action Committee.

> [The church] stands before the world as institution, while the world surges forward in movement. Institutions speak for those who have, while movement speaks for those who need. Institutions speak for status quo; movements for change, rapid change, or revolution. Institutions speak only for those who control them; movements for those who are controlled by institutions.

He reminds us of the urgency to change the church from institution to movement in order that it might link its potential power with the life of man in the city. He reminds us that the labor unions have become institutions; even the civil rights movement has stalled as it has become institutionalized. The church may be facing its last chance to prove that the Christian message is meaningful to man as he poises on the edge of a new leap forward.

We must listen to men like Jake McCarthy! He is not asking that the institutional church be abandoned, but he is asking for it to become a movement of Christian humanists who will penetrate all the sectors of the community. He is pleading for that dynamic community within the church to break the locks on the church doors and burst out upon life! This means that, paradoxically, there must be new forms of flexible organization to serve as the machinery for the task.

The Iona Community set up certain requirements for joining the community and developed a simple, flexible organizational structure to make the community a reality. The same must happen in local churches. This may cause the demise of such sacred groups as women's organizations or men's clubs. A simple, single board, may have to be substituted for a complex church government. Perhaps a church will release some of its key members and permit them to form a cell or community which will be charged with the responsibility for experimentation and avant-garde involvement in those areas of life where the gospel can be transformed into human, loving action.

The Old Cambridge Baptist Church, of Cambridge, Massachusetts, under the capable leadership of its pastor, the Reverend Ernst Klein, has sought church renewal and community penetration by organizing the church into task forces which are responsible for invading important sectors of life in Cambridge and environs. The annual yearbooks of this church are an inspiration as they describe the concerns for the various communities within the community of Cambridge. The task forces are themselves communities of lay people who are seeking to communicate the good news to individuals and through sociological structures of business, politics, education, leisure, and housing. One of my own staff members, Mrs. Carol Kolsti, belonged to one of these task forces or communities in which she found personal spiritual renewal, as well as new meaning for the church in the world.

One important thing to note, however, is the way in which these task forces rose spontaneously and how quickly they could be replaced as new needs emerged.

> It is significant to see how the task forces arose and what sanction they have in the life of the church. The church did not establish committees and then look for a purpose to justify their existence. Rather the church, sometimes through two or three alert laymen, discovered human needs; and to meet those needs a task force arose. The needs developed almost unpredictably from the events of the community — the arrival of refugees from Cuba, the civil rights movement, the crisis in urban renewal, the tidal wave of juvenile delinquency, the high incidence of men who return to prison after once being released. In most instances the task forces arose spontaneously, without formal approval of the church, but later were recognized by the church and were authorized by the coordinating committee to submit periodic reports to the church in its meetings.[3]

Articulation of Beliefs Which Discipline and Guide

It is an incontrovertible truth that belief in the Christian way of life must be linked with action. The seemingly new idea that action must precede reflection does not alter this truth. No one in his right mind would deny that much of the

[3] Stagg, op. cit., p. 92.

apathy of nominal church members (called *God's Frozen People* by Mark Gibbs and T. Ralph Morton) is due to the lack of any intensive, disciplined, mind-stretching, soul-searching quest for truth by those who took upon themselves the mantle of the great Teacher of Galilee. And here again, the Sunday school and other such organizations within the local church have been unable to bring this about because *they have been aiming at the whole constituency* instead of concentrating on the responsive few!

In every church there are people desiring to really plunge into the Bible and discover the theological truths which will help to answer their questions which have arisen out of their involvement in today's world. Among the hopeful signs of renewal in the church is the numerical growth of groups of such people. But, except for such movements as the Yokefellows, there is very little guidance and help available to either a pastor or a lay person who wants to spend time in theological study and social involvement.

One of the greatest needs today is the formation of lay academies or institutes which will help churches to pool resources and train cooperatively those key people who would then return to their churches and give guidance to the reconciling community in studying the world and in articulating common beliefs. All too much of the present format of Bible study groups consists of the pooling of corporate ignorance and cultic prejudices. The various national denominational agencies for Christian education as well as the avant-garde movements of the church can supply help in this direction.

Dietrich Bonhoeffer has said:

The Christian lives wholly by the truth of God's Word in Jesus Christ. If somebody asks him, Where is your salvation, your righteousness? he can never point to himself. He points to the Word of God in Jesus Christ, which assures him salvation and righteousness. He is as alert as possible to this Word. Because he daily hungers and thirsts for righteousness, he daily desires the redeeming Word. . . .

But God has put this Word into the mouth of men in order that it may be communicated to other men. When one person is struck by the Word, he speaks it to others. God has willed that we should seek him and find His living Word in the witness of a brother, in the mouth of man. Therefore, the Christian needs another Christian who speaks God's Word to him. He needs him again and again when he becomes uncertain and discouraged, for by himself he cannot help himself without belying the truth.[4]

One of the reasons why so many Christians have failed to join in the new reformation of the institutional church and the new thrusts into the community in which they live is that they have been confused over the very problem of the articulation of their faith and the verbalization of their beliefs. They have been led to believe that involvement at any of the levels of modern society must be in complete silence and without the speaking of the Word. Not that they are so anxious to communicate the Word to the hip generation, or the persons consumed by secularism; but at least they have the haunting feeling *that some word is expected,* and they don't know what to say, or whether to try to say anything at all!

The early Christian community discovered the power of words as good news to those who needed it. Significant contemporary Christian communities, such as the Lay Academy movement which began at Bad Boll, Germany, the Industrial Mission thrust of Mainz-Kastel, or the Detroit and Boston Industrial Missions, have used varied approaches but each has *articulated the word* in the context of contemporary needs.

In every local church there are people who want to speak the words, but they do not know how, or they are fearful of being misunderstood, or they have the idea that the gospel must only be proclaimed by life and not by lip. David Sheppard of the Mayflower Community reminds us that it is just as ridiculous to say by life and not by lip as to say by lip and not by life.

---

[4] Bonhoeffer, *op. cit.*, pp. 22-23.

Dietrich Bonhoeffer is often quoted as the one who urges religionless Christianity, but in *Life Together* he writes:

> The basis upon which Christians can speak to one another is that each knows the other as a sinner, who, with all his human dignity, is lonely and lost if he is not given help. This is not to make him contemptible nor to disparage him in any way. On the contrary, it is to accord him the one real dignity that man has, namely, that, though he is a sinner, he can share in God's grace and glory and be God's child. This recognition gives to our brotherly speech the freedom and candor that it needs. We speak to one another on the basis of the help *we both need*. We admonish one another to go the way that Christ bids us to go.[5]

Here is the clue to verbalization of God's truth in the midst of social action! We speak not for God to men, but with God among men! We speak as sinners who need to hear our own voices. We speak not as the pious to the lost, but as the penitent confessing his own needs. This is the kind of articulation that the world will hear and accept.

If the formation of beliefs and the articulation of those beliefs is one of the fundamental bases of the reconciling community, *worship* is the breath which brings life to that body. The Sunday morning worship experience may be the one place where the *dynamic* is *initiated* for this formulation of beliefs, but the small group experiencing the glowing aspects of the "two or three gathered in my name" will do more to fan the flames than any other one factor.

The secret of the Iona Community is found in the reformation of its liturgy for the large worship services and in the formation of small groups for the purpose of strengthening individuals through face-to-face prayer and confession. Dr. MacLeod has written in *We Shall Re-build:*

> Let a congregation stop short at the first, glorying only that it has been taken out of the world, and it will soon come under the con-

[5] *Ibid.,* pp. 105-106 (italics ours).

demnation of the man who, being given a talent, buried it in the earth. Let a congregation luxuriate only in the second activity, in the elaboration of its services and the rigour of its discipline, and it will soon come under the condemnation of those who stored up the manna lest no manna should fall next day: The very materials of its nourishment will go bad on them. Or let a congregation be for ever running missions, concentrating only on the outsider, counting as indifferent both the state of their own redemption and the methods of its constant nourishment, and it, in its turn, will find soon enough that it has hewn out broken cisterns that hold no water.[6]

The Iona Community issues a prayer card which is used as a common guide for private prayer. Each member covenants to pray daily at a common, fixed time. Within any local congregation a small group, including the pastor, could prepare its own techniques for prayer, goals for prayer, times for prayer, and quietly and effectively carry these out.

The Baptist City Society of Boston, like so many other city mission societies in major cities of the United States, has a camp which is utilized each summer to make it possible for city children to get off the streets and have a week or two in the woods in an atmosphere of Christian influences. One year I served as director of a camp of forty junior-aged children from the Boston area.

Camp started out with a bang when three eleven-year-old boys started to slip away from the central area. They were intercepted by a staff person who discovered that one of the boys had an older brother in a nearby penitentiary and the three young heroes were going "to spring him out because he was framed." Two of these boys soon distinguished themselves as troublemakers who were tough, defiant, and unmanageable.

Most Christian camps are approximate models of the Christian community. They have "persons" there who have been gripped by the person of Christ and because of this many a

[6] George MacLeod, *We Shall Re-build* (Glasgow: Iona Community, Publishing Department, n.d.), p. 24.

church young person and even a nonchurch youth has been influenced toward a radical change of life. Because camp life entails living together in community with a sense of the presence of Christ, many people have had spiritual experiences during camp which continue to influence them for years. This is what we were hoping would happen in the lives of these city children as they walked trails, splashed in the swimming pool, sang around the fireplace, and worshiped in the chapel.

Having the central theme of this book in mind, I wanted most of all to discover whether or not I could communicate with these children. Could I verbalize the Christian faith in an understandable way to children who came from ghettos, broken homes, and a churchless existence? It seemed very dubious.

Each vesper service I led was based on Carl Burke's book *God Is for Real, Man.* All I did was involve some of the children in the vespers by asking them to read simple passages of Scripture, and then I read from *God Is for Real, Man* the same passage in contemporary language which they understood, and added a brief explanation of Christian truth.

Following one vesper service when I had read the section entitled "A Party for Junior," which was the story of the prodigal son told in the language of inner-city kids, my two eleven-year-old troublemakers, Nathan and Tom, came up to me and said they would like to say something. We walked off toward the woods and sat on a rock. Then Nathan said, "We want to tell you we're sorry for the way we've been acting." That was all they said, but all three of us had tears in our eyes as I put my arms around them in the act of forgiveness. From that time forward these were changed boys! They didn't have halos on and crises still arose, but they were different. What happened? The change was the effect of the Christian community — the caring counselor, the loving lifeguard, the patient craft teacher; each of them reflected the Person who loves now, even as he did on the shores of Galilee. The truth of God's love and forgiveness become incarnate in three lives. What happened? Two confused little boys who have been knocked about in life and were seeking some awareness of their own selfhood responded to the Father's call. Most of all, it was the coming of the kingdom for three of us, and that's what the Christian community is all about.

❖❖❖ A TACTICAL PLAN
FOR THE RECONCILING COMMUNITY

AT NATIONAL CONFERENCES, state gatherings, or in local groups the main topic under discussion is the renewal of the church — how to bring new life to the institutional church and particularly how to retool the church for the urbanized age in which we live. But there is too much talk about the problem and too little discussion of the techniques for bringing about the needed changes. For this reason church members who care are growing tired of being inspired toward renewal and then frustrated because nothing much ever seems to happen to fulfill their inspired hopes.

In the first chapters I have indicated the struggle which is going on in the church between the traditionalists and the experimentalists over the question of how to renew the church. I have suggested that better utilization of the inner remnant of the church as the reconciling community is a place to begin. But given a small dedicated group of people who are willing to be the cutting edge of the church in the world, the question still arises: Where do we go from here?

Moving from Research to Tactics

Most major denominations and countless councils of churches are trying to answer the question "Where do we go from here?" with departments of research and strategy. These are essential in any organization which will survive this age. There is a new interest in long-range planning, and even local churches have committees for this purpose. The twentieth-century religious leader is aware of the place in his community of the professional planner, and he likewise knows how essential it is for his church to forecast the future and be ready for the changes which will be demanded of it. But, in the imagery used by George MacLeod, we can have the church walls lined with battle maps and strategies and never get out to the actual battle with our development of tactics. Strategy is the development of the large overall plan, while tactics are the maneuvering of the troops in specific situations. One of the reasons why so many church people are tired of the talk about church renewal is that they never get to the actual battle.

The reconciling community, then, should become a tactical unit with special assignments which only it can carry out. As the leader of the tactical unit, the minister of the smaller church will have problems. Some members of the parish will want him to give his time to the inconsequential things like running the mimeograph machine, visiting all the members frequently, and raising the finances of the church so it can keep going. One possible solution to this problem is the formation of a team ministry, where several churches might be willing to federate or unite, thus freeing one of the men to lead the reconciling community as a tactical unit in a unique encounter in the world. The other men could take care of the preaching and other household chores of the church.

The larger and more affluent church may decide to depart

from the traditional multiple-staff assignments and employ a man to lead the remnant of the concerned into community involvement. The First Baptist Church of Worcester, Massachusetts, has moved in this direction with the addition of two ministers to their staff with non-traditional responsibilities to lead the church into new forms of ministry. One of the ministers is responsible for teaching the laity to think theologically concerning their place in the world. The other is released to the community and may not even be in the church on a given Sunday. But he is the one who guides the church and the reconciling community within it through the development of a tactical approach to the city. However it is done, in order to survive and to be faithful to its reason for being, the church must make its choice between spending its strength on constant preparation for battle or on the battlefield in actual hand-to-hand struggle.

The Training for Tactics

A crucial question is: "Who will train the people who offer themselves as the reconciling community?" Sadly, the average parish minister is not able to carry out this function. His seminary has done little to prepare him for this role. Many seminary students working in Christian centers or in inner-city churches have said to me, "I'm not prepared for what I'm discovering in this community."

This situation indicates then that there must be a whole new development of training centers for those who would like to step out in daring mission in the world. The Ecumenical Institute of Chicago might very well be the model or even one of the actual agents for doing this. Denominations have been slow to recognize the potential in the Ecumenical Institute's approach to training clergymen and laymen for being the church in word and deed. In a brochure published by the Institute, Dean Joseph Mathews is asked, "Just what do you do at the Ecumenical Institute?" He answers:

The program of the Institute is rooted in the new image of the church as mission. We call ourselves "Structural Revolutionaries" because we are unreservedly dedicated to the principle that the church is renewable from within. The new sense of mission in the church is the context for all our activities.

The local congregation in every situation is the focal point for our work. It is the place where everyday decisions are made, life styles forged and the world most directly and significantly touched.

Today the People of God at the grassroots are the new "elite" in history — from them will come a disciplined body of churchmen. They must become theologically equipped and practically enabled to be the church in word and deed.

These insights and convictions set the stage for answering the question "What does the Ecumenical Institute do?"

Our role is to aid in the renewal of the church for the sake of all civilization. Our strategy is three-fold:

1. TRAINING The Ecumenical Institute, founded from a resolution of the Second Assembly of the World Council of Churches, is a comprehensive research and training center. We provide laymen and clergymen with the intellectual tools and the practical model-building skills which every awakened man needs. Our methods and curricula evoke a latent Christian memory and enable participants to appropriate the contemporary cultural wisdom. Both jobs must be done simultaneously. Over 60,000 persons were touched by the program of the Institute last year. Some 16,000 were directly involved in the curriculum as it was taught by the faculty across the nation and throughout the world.

2. COMMUNITY REFORMULATION Our inner city project goes beyond all previous approaches to community reorganization. We are attempting to build a model which will be applicable to every urban area across the world. In a limited geographical area we deal with all of the problems of all of the people. Crucial to this is the depth human problem — the way a man sees himself in the world — . In Chicago's West Side ghetto, the resident operates out of a victim image.

Wherever authentic human community is to emerge, new images of human significance must be consciously created and forcefully dramatized. This is what we mean by "imaginal education"— motivating a person to come to terms with his depth human problem. Adequate self-images offer the deep awareness of individual significance, personal integrity, and vocational accomplishment. They endow the human imagination with those pictures that allow a man to appropriate his own unique gift to history.

3. RESEARCH The 200 persons who are the faculty of the Institute work as a research team. New curricula, materials and procedures for the training of adults, youth and children are constantly being developed. New models of the family, new forms for public, family and private worship are tested by the faculty, corporately and individually. Bound together under a common covenant, the faculty is an experimental "family order" discovering what it means to be a disciplined body of people for the sake of the mission of the church. By sharing meals and facilities, living costs are cut to a minimum. By living at the center of our mission in the West Side ghetto, we are constantly involved with those with whom we work. By supporting ourselves financially, every penny that is given to the Institute goes directly into the mission. By living in covenant, we are accountable to each other for the particular aspects of the mission.

Our world, secular-scientific-urban, is a radically new historical arena. This brand new world demands a new life style — religious-secular, disciplined, practical, and profoundly human.[1]

I would like to call attention to two statements from Mr. Mathews' response. The first is: "Our methods and curricula evoke a latent Christian memory and enable participants to appropriate the contemporary cultural wisdom." The Christian community must begin with biblical and theological training in the light of the age in which it serves. It must learn to translate the Bible into the language which people speak and to deal with the whole man in the whole community according to the very best techniques available.

The second emphasis is the building of a model. Though books are being written to describe churches which are experiencing renewal, very few of us are attempting to build our own models of Christian community where we are. But this we must do.

Let me illustrate this through sharing the story of changes taking place in the Bethel Christian Center of Boston. Traditionally, the Bethel Christian Center has been a social center

[1] From a brochure of The Ecumenical Institute, 3444 Congress Parkway, Chicago, Illinois 60624.

staffed by a professional missionary staff. Located in the North End of Boston, a predominantly Roman Catholic, Italian community, it has had a long history as an institution based in a hostile community for the purpose of mission. Its program has been made up of nursery school for children, clubs for children and youth, ceramic groups, art classes, modern dance, and other usual functions of such a center. But the Center, at least in its latter days, was not a model of Christian community. Attempts had been made by the professional staff to relate to the community, to establish a worshiping congregation, but all to little avail. Then, with the turnover of staff the entire group of professional missionaries was replaced with two seminary students (one from a seminary considered to be liberal and one from a seminary considered to be conservative), a hotel receptionist, a school teacher, and a conscientious objector who had been in the Vista program and was himself a community organizer. This group became what Dean Mathews called a "family order," "bound together under a common covenant . . . discovering what it means to be a disciplined body of people for the sake of the mission of the church." These are church people living in the North End because they have a concern for people. The first week they were there the school teacher's car had all its tires punctured, but he was undaunted. An amazing development was that he was invited to become a school teacher in the Roman Catholic High School across the street from the Center. This was the first time in history that such a breakthrough in the community was made by someone from the Center.

The members of the Bethel community have drawn up a discipline for themselves. As "the gathered" in a hostile community they go out onto the street and get to know the people. As residents of the community who do not have a set, stereotyped program but who are concerned out of Christ-motivated love, they are attempting to relate to the community organizations located there.

Some will ask, "What's this got to do with my local church?" Just this — it can serve as a model. No one can develop a handbook for churches to which one may turn to find specific instructions for changeover. But if a group will have the daring and abandon of the early church, or of the Ecumenical Institute, it may well launch out in some unique way in its own community.

The Reconciling Community in the Pluralistic Church

Just as the world we live in is no longer a simple world revolving around a rurally-oriented economy with the local church at its center, so the church is no longer a simple church. It is pluralistic with manifestations of its body at all levels of life.

The Underground Church

Malcolm Boyd, the so-called "night club priest," in appearing on Boston's City Mission Society television program told the audience of his discovery of a tremendously latent church in the most unlikely places. He calls this the "underground church." Many periodical articles have been written about this hidden remnant; and there may be an underground church that has no previous nor present relationship with the contemporary institutional church.

There is also a latent, underground church *within the institution,* which is idle, angry, and silent. Its members see little reason for church attendance except on rare occasions and are even diverting resources of talent and finances to other areas of activity. One sharp, dedicated young man I know who headed a major board in his church dropped out of all activities of this nature because he thought it a waste of his time and energy.

While traveling in Europe I met such people almost daily. One couple had lived in France for two years and were returning to the United States. When they learned I was a minister from Boston, they approached me and asked if I had gone to Selma during the crisis there. When I assured them I had been there, they extended their hands and said, "You're the kind of churchman we want to know." Then they went on to tell me of their respective church affiliations and how they had not been inside a church for over three years. They made it clear that they were Christians with a concern for the real, basic issues of life. They didn't want to waste themselves on the turning of church-machinery wheels, neither did they want their spiritual leader to mouth innocuous thoughts before an applauding people. Then they asked me the tough question, "Where in Boston is there such a minister and such a church?" Where could they join with others who have this same discriminating desire to practice what Christian faith means?

Whenever I mention the underground church, I find people in the church who want to establish contact with like-minded individuals within the church and outside it. They ask, "How can I get in touch with others who believe this way?"

Perhaps each major city and town could establish a type of evangelical lay academy, remembering that the German academies insist upon a majority of nonchurch people present at any particular training conference. A community might well agree to have one less church in existence and turn that building over for the establishment of a lay-training center where those from the underground church could meet with others of a like mind and form a community. Out of this the churches would receive a leaven and a change-agent to move the whole church toward action. These underground members, as another community of faith, might develop a significant relationship in worship and action which must even take place outside the established churches but would have their blessing and support.

The Surface Church

The "surface church" is that group of local parishes which

meet on Sunday morning for worship, Christian education, and fellowship. Each of the parishes in the surface church has a unique and distinct personality. Some are young churches thriving with large congregations in new suburban developments; some are older churches located in inner suburbia, or the outer city, but now experiencing pains of occasional arthritis as congregations continue to hold their own, but the ministers and their sensitive leaders feel the pangs of old age and look for ways of renewal. Then there are the old, old churches left as dying derelicts in the inner city or the abandoned rural area. The struggling groups remaining with these churches have problems in maintaining rapidly deteriorating buildings. Their financial resources are less and less each year, and their prospects for the future are as dismal. How does one conceive of the reconciling community in the surface church with all its various types of expression of the Christian way?

The first consideration must be *the neighborhood of the local church.* One of the problems related to the emphasis on neighborhood ministries springs from the parochial concept of the neighborhood as that limited land around the church building, be it city blocks, suburban developments, or small-town farm lands. It may be any one of these, but it may be more. The local neighborhood of the local church now spans miles through subways, bus routes, and highways. It has become the larger community with all of its political, cultural, and sociological problems. But the neighborhood also begins right where the church is located.

Several women of a city church became concerned about the children who played on the street only to be chased away by well-meaning policemen. It occurred to these women that rather than chase these kids away from the front of their church they might very well find a way to open the church's doors so that the children had a place to play. They established contact with a local city mission society and were trained in neighborhood ministry. This led to the organization of simple club groups which met on weekdays for the purpose of recreation. The women who had the concern became the groups' leaders, and a simple, elementary reconciling community was born.

Many sophisticated church renewal experts will look askance at such a simple, local neighborhood ministry concept as too little among too few. But we have to start where people are, and this concept of a weekday ministry to those living in the immediate area may be the beginning of a larger concept. The Boston Baptist City Mission Society staff developed a suggested Neighborhood Ministries philosophy around which a group of concerned could gather and move to action. It is as follows:

Our Neighborhood Ministries program, from the very beginning of the program, has been a pioneering effort that has proven to have significant value. As other cities have followed our leading they have also added from their own experience to the wealth of possibilities for service under this general idea. Now, we too are ready to expand our own concept of Neighborhood Ministries into a concept which adds to the children's club program that we have pioneered. This we are calling our fourfold approach to Neighborhood Ministries.

I. NEIGHBORHOOD CLUBS

Group work services including children's clubs, clubs for youth and older people, special interest activities, etc., conducted both at the Bethel Christian Center and in the churches of the inner city are conducted with the following goals: (1) to show the church's concern for the person by providing opportunities to fill their leisure with constructive activity; (2) to deal directly with the emotional and spiritual needs of the participants in the club program; (3) to identify social and material needs of the participants and their families and to help fulfill these needs or to refer them to sources of fulfillment; (4) to make Christ known through "incarnational" witness.

II. NEIGHBORHOOD INVOLVEMENT

To meet the vast needs of today's urban population, organization of the community has been necessary so that the resources available can be obtained at the place of need. Thus, in nearly every community there are several kinds of community organizations. It is part of our Christian responsibility to the "leaven" in the structures of the community. We are prepared to be a resource guide — and goad if need be — to the churches, helping them to relate to the real needs of their own neighborhood. We will help them to relate to existing organizations or to initiate organization where it is needed.

III. NEIGHBORHOOD RESOURCES

In every community, and for the city as a whole, there are resources to meet nearly every existing need. Often we are not aware of the resources and the rights of those who need them. We hope, therefore, to be a source of information to help churches and individuals to find the resources to meet each particular need. We hope to be able to lead people to the resources and follow them through to see that their needs are permanently relieved.

IV. NEIGHBORHOOD FACILITIES

Facilities for housing, social services, etc., for the elderly and the underprivileged are being encouraged not only by social service agencies, but the loan facilities of the government are available for the provision of these needs. Our aim is to encourage the churches to get involved in these projects. It is possible that in some cases our own resources will be used toward developing such facilities.[2]

Each surface church has to appraise itself and ask how it can begin to develop a community of concern in its particular place? One aspect of meaningful service for local churches has been strangely overlooked by the church. I refer to the idea of voluntary services, new, ecumenical, fresh instruments for those who want to serve in the community but outside the church walls. They want to be more than deacons mending fences by visiting malcontents who are unhappy with the minister. They have a concern for the lonely, forgotten, dispossessed, and unloved. Unfortunately the denominations and even councils of churches have not been of much help in guiding churches into the utilization of volunteers. I know of no national or state church agencies which have a department charged with this specific responsibility. Yet, there are cries for help from community organizations which could

[2] Neighborhood Ministries Staff, Boston Baptist Bethel City Mission Societies, "Philosophy of Neighborhood Ministries."

open the way for the incarnational involvement of members from local parishes. The City Missionary Society of Boston (United Church of Christ) has pioneered in this respect. Their Department of Voluntarism has guided thousands of church people into direct participation in the relocation of families in urban renewal area. They have related concerned church people to prisons, hospitals, and nursing homes.

Some churches have found the idea of the FISH movement to be a means of channeling the energies and commitment of their members. (The name FISH is based upon the early Christian use of a fish as a symbol for Christ. The symbolism grows out of the fact that in Greek the initial letters of "Jesus Christ, God's Son, Savior" spell the word "fish.") The first branch of FISH was formed in 1961 at the Anglican Church of St. Andrew in Oxford, England. The first FISH group in the United States was organized in West Springfield, Massachusetts, by the Reverend Robert L. Howell, rector of the Episcopal Church of the Good Shepherd. With a staff of fifty volunteers on call around the clock, West Springfield's FISH has been able to help people in countless small human ways. One example — when a man with five children discovered that his wife was fatally ill, FISH volunteers took turns cooking meals for the family, doing the laundry, and continued helping out for several weeks after the wife's death until the family could make other arrangements.

FISH undertakes any reasonable request where a genuine need exists. For example, after one tearful high school student asked FISH to help explain a poor report card to his father, a sympathetic parent and member of FISH actually escorted the boy home and helped break the bad news to dad!

The Melrose Highlands Congregational Church picked up this idea of FISH program from Springfield and invited the community to become a part of it. It began functioning with a twenty-four hour telephone service which was advertised in the local press. Handbills were also distributed throughout the city informing people of this service. They made it clear to the community that any emergency which fell within the scope of FISH would be met; otherwise a FISH volunteer would contact the local police, doctor, visiting nurse, Red Cross, clergyman, or other appropriate agency. FISH operates on a seven-day week and twenty-four hour schedule with a nucleus of volunteers on call. A large number of these are couples who are willing to go out together on a night call. Another aspect of this program was the establishment of the "Fish Lines." In each Fish Line there are eight persons who live alone. One calls the next in line each day at a specified time, and the eighth reports back to FISH that all calls have been completed. This chain of human kindness provides needed contact for lonely persons, and it is reported that in at least one case a man's life was saved. A man who was a member of a Fish Line in Marshfield, Massachusetts, failed to answer his phone one day. This was reported to the FISH volunteer of the day, who went to the man's house with the police and discovered that he had suffered a severe stroke.

There are many groups of Christians in local churches who would like to form as another community or a FISH program but are kept from doing so by the existing cumbersome structure of the surface church which discourages breaking out into new forms of ministry. Another factor is the church building, which requires maintenance, repairs, updating of furniture and equipment. All add heavy overhead costs to the constituency; worse than that, the energies of good people are dissipated on the church building and its related problems rather than in a community through witness and work.

The time has come for some daring experimentation in solving this problem. One answer might be the concentration of resources and equipment in a cathedral-church which would be central in a given neighborhood area and would make unnecessary other church buildings in that same area. A worship center adaptable to all faiths at the heart of a multi-service building would testify to the community of Christian unity as well as economy of time and money.

Urban renewal in the Roxbury, Washington Park area of Boston removed several church buildings, and the denominational leadership took the initiative to insist that instead of restoring three or four churches as separate denominational units there could be a new Ecumenical Center. Today the Ecumenical Center in Roxbury affirms in its by-laws:

> In our own time, God is calling mankind humbly to recognize the sinfulness of its divisiveness. No one, not even the church, can escape guilt for this sin. The Ecumenical Center in Roxbury is a coming together of Christians and men of good will to serve the present and shape the future of Roxbury and the neighboring community. Through this effort the church as Servant of all men will attempt to re-affirm human dignity, to discover new forms of common life and to share the concerns of the community that its members have every opportunity to live in freedom, justice and love.

Out of this philosophy of ecumenical mission has grown the Ecumenical Center of Roxbury which will be housed in a functional, million-dollar building which will be constructed for the purpose of meeting all the needs of the whole community rather than some of the needs of one particular denomination.

In Brookline, Massachusetts, three strong churches have made a very historic decision. The Baptist Church, Harvard Church (U.C.C.), and St. Mark's Methodist Church voted to form a united parish where joint strategic planning and utilization of buildings would cut down on financial overhead and at the same time provide for a unified approach to the community. Youth groups, church school, and other special gatherings meet in one building while worship services are held in the other buildings on a rotating basis. These first steps in daring to settle the problems related to the maintenance of three large buildings are only the beginning of what may be the formation of a new parish-team approach in the midst of the city. With the sharing of staff and the creation of a small ecumenical Christian community as a task force concerned for the larger community, The Brookline United Parish may be pioneering for the rest of us.

Flexibility is the key to making needed changes in the life of the surface church. Whoever said that worship ought to be always at eleven o'clock on Sunday morning? Most of us have forgotten that this hour was chosen in the day of a rural economy because this was a time when all the farm chores were completed. We still treat this sacred hour as though it was ordered by our Lord himself. Services of worship should be held at times when people are able to come together. Some experimentation is being done in this area. Worship services are being held at midweek hours such as 6 A.M. on Thursday for those who can't make it on Sunday.

One of the greatest stumbling blocks to flexibility in the surface church is the complex organizational structure which requires hours of time and energy from overworked people. For example, a church of thirty-seven members drew up a new constitution and by-laws which called for sixty-three officers and committee members. Is it any wonder that church people are too tired to break out into meaningful forms of mission? Some churches, large and small, should be willing to declare a moratorium on all committees and boards for one to three years. A simple executive council could be formed and each member of the council could be charged with the responsibility for one area of church organization. For example, one could be the person responsible for the building, another for Christian education, another for music, another for finances, and so on. Some churches have tried this and have found it to be effective.

The Christ Church Presbyterian of Burlington, Vermont, deserves a special citation for its valor in courageously facing some of these problems which keep a people from relating in significant mission to a community. This church was organized in 1955 at the invitation of the Burlington Council of Churches. Some thirty to sixty members started out with high expectations. They purchased seven acres of land, a house for the minister, and a TV store which was made into a temporary chapel. The congregation is still meeting in the temporary store chapel. These services are held only once a month; the seven acres of land are for sale; but the church has a dynamic program of community outreach. This is a case of a young church deciding that every member would be a vital part of the reconciling community. For six nights a week the members are busy operating The Loft, a coffee house and bookstore which they own in the heart of the Burlington business district. Each night of the week there are task-force operations such as visiting the prisoners of the county jail. In addition to this the same callers visit with judges, probation officers, and wives of inmates. The women of the church visit the Lund Home for unwed mothers. Other members relate to social issues as they arise — circulating petitions for low-income housing, sponsoring political debates, or meeting with the mayor to talk about youth recreation facilities. Once a week for a period of twelve weeks, prospective members meet with the teaching elder (pastor) in a church membership class. Once a month the entire congregation gathers for a rousing all-day period of worship, study, celebration, and a planning session.

In June of 1966 the church drew up a significant document which expresses the philosophy underlying its program:

It is proposed that the normative institutional structure of Christ Church Presbyterian be defined by the pragmatic forms in which the church finds itself in mission. In other words, the Loft, Lund Home, Jail, Occupational and other groups are Christ Church Presbyterian. We have only to grant them the freedom (time, for example) to authentically carry out the liturgical functions of service, worship, and study.

In order that they may be so freed, we propose that the Sunday exercises presently practiced be abandoned. Instead of weekly worship at 10:30 a.m., we propose that each mission group consider and carry out a form and time of worship appropriate to that particular mission. Instead of a standard period of study each Sunday night for all, we propose that each mission group consider and carry out a form of study that is necessary and appropriate to that particular mission. And instead of an hour of church school for our children each week, we propose that religious education be structured around and oriented to the realistic child centers of home and school, and, to the extent possible, to the church where it is in mission.

Because we remain one Body, in Christ, it is proposed that all members and participants gather together on the first Sunday of each month for an open-ended and relatively unstructured meeting. The purpose of the monthly meeting would be for communication, strategy, redirection, study, and celebration.[3]

This church is teaching us to see the church as the people of God in mission in the world, the leaven in the lump, the salt of the earth, the reconciling community in the larger community. It conceives of the surface church not as the headquarters from which the gospel is sent out but as the actual body of our Lord taking upon itself the suffering and hurt of people, the sin and ignorance of the wayward. This is incarnational evangelism, making Christ known in word and flesh.

The Elevated Church

The World Council of Churches had two study groups meeting simultaneously to prepare reports on the "Missionary Structure of the Congregation." One of these groups was composed of Europeans and met in major centers of that continent. In the meantime the North American members met in representative regions of the United States. In these conferences many questions were raised, such as: "What kind of institutions are needed on a national level? What national 'problems' and 'structures' are there which call for Christian presence?

[3] *The Church for Others* (Geneva: World Council of Churches, 1967), p. 129.

How are these to be related to regional and local changes?" But no answers were suggested and the study groups steered away from the vital question of reshaping the elevated church composed of denominational and ecumenical organizations!

Not enough attention has been given to the matter of the linkage between the surface and elevated church. It has been assumed that involvement, reshaping, revitalization of the church of Christ is something national, state, and city denominational agencies recommend for the local congregations, but do not apply to themselves. Yet, much of what hinders reformation in the surface church is the very rigidity of elevated, denominational structures.

The North American working group for the W.C.C. did raise the question of why national denominational agencies had chosen the *commercial model* as their "model" for reorganization. Have they chosen the business model for efficiency or financial reasons? Why did they not choose the political model, or the educational model, or the communications model? Do not these latter models have more in common with the church than does the business world?

The purpose of this part of the discussion is not to come to grips with the reshaping of the elevated church at the national level but to suggest that the most exciting and opportune level for reshaping the elevated church today is at the metropolitan level. Gibson Winter in his *The Suburban Captivity of the Churches* warned that major Protestant denominations are still rurally oriented even though those denominations are becoming more and more metropolitan in character. Because growing suburbia seemed to offer potential financial resources, the denominations concentrated on metropolitan perimeters and forsook the centers. Now, with the coming of riots and destruction, the failure to approach the metropolitan complex as a totality is evident. This has resulted in alienation not only between churches of the outer city and the inner, but between the people of these respective districts.

The metropolitan sections of the United States now contain well over 60 percent of the total population. Some of these clusters have three to six million, or even as many as twenty-three million inhabitants. The problems arising out of this new kind of urbanized life are almost inconceivable. But one thing is certain, things are in a mess! The problems of government, transportation, air-pollution, education, housing, and other such items call for new metro-political superstructures. Perhaps what Toronto did in establishing the municipality of metropolitan Toronto in 1953 is relevant to our situation. Miraculously thirteen municipalities became part of a federal system of local governments. Could this political model also say something to the elevated church? If cities and towns can come together, keeping something of local autonomy, but pooling resources and strengths to solve problems of the metropolitan region, why cannot the denominations? In this type of relationship the reconciling community could find expression through the elevated church.

A new kind of metropolitan manifestation of community is appearing in the United States which promises to provide an instrumentality for the gathering and the dispersing of the reconciling community in mission. In 1965 under the leadership of Dr. David Barry, thirty denominational executives met in New York City to pledge their cooperation in JOINT ACTION FOR MISSION. In 1966 the denominational leaders of the Boston area invited Dr. Barry to visit them and explain JAM to them and key leaders from their constituency. While this idea was catching on in Chicago, Rochester, Cleveland, Syracuse, Toledo, Delaware, and Los Angeles, the executives of the city mission societies in Boston met in retreats to consider a possible plan for action in the metropolitan area. They finally agreed upon a covenant which was presented to their respective boards for action. The text of it follows:

This year, 1967, the various denominational organizations which are charged with the responsibility for mission in the various sectors of Metropolitan Boston gathered to officially adopt a covenant for Joint Action for Mission. This Covenant reads as follows:

"Believing that the multiple social, economic, and religious needs of an urban society cannot be met by any one agency or denomination; that the complexity of these problems calls for the greatest skills and dedication available; and recognizing that these skills and the dedication are available in the many interested and involved individuals and groups now working in these fields, we, the undersigned, join in covenant relationship, under God, for joint action for mission within Metropolitan Boston.

We would hope, by such united, cooperative action, to conserve and capitalize upon all designated moneys, personal knowledge, and skills represented in this covenanting body.

We would hope, also, that such a united effort shall give one voice, strong enough and powerful enough to be heard in the various political, educational, social, economic, and religious power structures of our city; and, having been heard, one body with hands to serve, feet to go, and minds and hearts of compassion to institute action that shall reclaim the TOTAL man, family, and community.

We recognize the individual character of the persons, agencies, and denominations involved; and further recognize that the various creeds, policies, and practices that make us different are the very things that can make us strong; and we would not intend to violate these by such a body, believing that the unity of such bodies shall set the example for joint action for mission in our community.

Therefore We Covenant Together Under God:

(1) To cooperate with each other, the community, and any and all persons or groups engaged in mission work within Metropolitan Boston.

(2) To seek and accept advice and counsel from all such aforesaid persons and groups.

(3) To coordinate personnel, time, program and finances to do the most effective ministry in as many areas of need as possible.

(4) To invite all others to join with us in this covenant as they indicate interest in urban mission.

(5) To be ready to dissolve this covenanting body at any time a more effective body might arise to perform what we believe to be a necessary service in mission to Boston.

We agree, in order that our Covenant should best be carried out, that we:

> Organize an official body to be known as the City Missionary Council with duly elected officers under such constitution as that body may devise within the meaning and purpose of this covenant."

This Covenant was adopted by the following respective organizations: The Baptist City Mission Society; the City Missionary Society of the United Church of Christ; the Episcopal City Mission Society; the Methodists, Presbyterians, and Salvation Army. The Unitarian Benevolent Society has been a cooperating agency in this program also.[4]

The following are existing programs where the various city denominational agencies are now working in cooperation with each other: (Not all the denominations are contributing money or staff to these programs, but in every case there is ecumenical involvement and in most cases participation in strategy and financial undergirding.)

The Columbia Point Chaplaincy: For more than six years the City Mission organizations have pooled financial resources to make a man available to the 6,000 residents of Columbia Point. Mr. William Loesch is serving effectively at this time. Since there is no Protestant church available in this immediate community, a Center has been established in a store front opposite the housing units. Out of this Center has emanated a community program run by the residents of the project including released time religious education, community improvement, adult Bible study, and corporate concern for human beings in trouble. Mr. Loesch has coordinated this program and won a real place in the hearts of the residents. A new venture has been a Sunday evening worship service in the Columbia Point Center.

The Ecumenical Center in Roxbury: The Ecumenical Center in Roxbury grew out of the proposed merger of two denominational service groups to a cooperative endeavor with all major denominations including Roman Catholic. From an original plan to build a proposed

---

[4] Joint Action for Mission in Metropolitan Boston, 1967, pp. 1-2.

$500,000 building, plans have now moved toward a $1,250,000 facility. The Center has grown from a club and day care program to a community organization component with block programs with children, Day-care, Head Start programs; a Health Center under joint sponsorship with Beth-Israel Hospital; a mental health program in cooperation with the Massachusetts Mental Health Association. The Center has been entrusted with the development of a Neighborhood Service project with a large grant for developing programs. The Center will be responsible for initiating these programs and turning them over to the community agencies for implementation.

The City Missionary Societies have made possible the employment of a full-time staff person at the Center. A minister from the United Church of Christ has just been called as full-time director.

The Boston Industrial Mission: The Boston Industrial Mission is led by executive director, the Rev. Scott Paradise, who served with the Sheffield Industrial Mission in England and the Detroit Industrial Mission in Michigan. The Rev. Norman Faramelli has recently come as associate director.

B.I.M. has focused its attention upon the Research and Development departments of the electronic industries surrounding Boston. In the light of the implications of the Christian Gospel, the B.I.M. has established contacts with men in these industries for the purpose of dialogue which will result in action concerning the relationship between technology and human values.

Groups of men have come together in these industries to informally discuss the human implications of their work, of their industrial organizations and of the new technological civilization we are creating. It is hoped that thoughts growing out of these discussions, aided by insights of faith, will enable the church and religious community to learn more about technologies [sic] thinking. This in turn will make communication between the religious world and the technological work possible.

Spanish Speaking Work: For several years the Spanish speaking Puerto-Ricans have been settling in Boston. The greatest concentration has been in the South End. The Episcopalians, Baptists and Salvation Army have staff persons with special responsibility to this community. The Spanish Speaking Center in the South End has been very much involved in court actions against slum-lords, and in seeking ways to enable the Puerto-Ricans to discover a way of life which will bring fulfillment.

Ministry with the Aging: With the increasing number of older adults in our urban society it has become increasingly necessary to find co-operative means by which church agencies can meet the problems created by an unpreparedness on the part of society to face this new aspect of American life.

Some of our organizations have staff persons with special expertise in working with the aging. All of us are facing the most serious problem which is the lack of adequate housing.

Campus Ministries: Several of our agencies share in the ministry of those who give themselves in the involvement of witness and action amongst the students of our metropolitan college campuses. Faculty and students alike have had great concern for the people caught in city ghettoes. They have been involved in tutoring programs and other action-oriented movements for the betterment of city conditions.

The Seventh Circle Coffee House is one manifestation of a new cooperative endeavor.

Blue Hill Christian Center: The Center at Blue Hill has been supported financially by the Baptists and Congregationalists, but has involved people of every denomination and faith. Being strategically located in the midst of the struggle for better housing, better schools and the uplifting of men, it has made significant strides in training indigenous leadership for the community.

The Opportunities Industrialization Center: O.I.C. is a hopeful expression of self determination. The black community has established this Center to train and retrain people for jobs. The City Missionary Societies are attempting to lend their support to O.I.C. without domination and control. Our greatest task lies ahead; the opening of opportunities for widespread employment is a top priority.

The Boston Industrial Mission has been working closely with O.I.C. in setting up meetings with men in Research and Development who in turn are helping to set up courses in electronics.[5]

Because there is no viable Protestant church instrumentality for carrying out a Joint Action for Mission program in metropolitan Boston, the various denominations under the guidance of the Massachusetts Council of Churches have formed a

[5] *Ibid.,* pp. 2-4.

Metropolitan Boston Commission which in its infancy is beginning to guide the churches in a significant program of Joint
Action for Mission. Building upon the strengths of the existing denominational programs, the Metropolitan Commission
is projecting programs for lay training in urban mission and
supervised urban training for seminary students. Church involvement in interfaith housing; involvement in programs for
the aging, for youth, and persons of special need; exciting
new forms of mission in housing projects, on campuses, in
prisons, in industrial complexes and other sectors of society
are being correlated and coordinated. Volunteer services in
cooperation with community organizations are coming into
being. For the first time in history, members of greater Boston
churches who really want guidance in forming their own tactics for mission can receive it through the JAM philosophy of
the Metropolitan Boston Commission. The *Report of the National Advisory Commission on Civil Disorder* (more commonly known as the Kerner Report) prompted the Commission to
assume the responsibility for addressing itself to the white
community of the metropolitan area, challenging it to end
racism, poverty, and injustice. The Commission has linked
with existing organizations that are attempting to do this and
serves as a conduit for the churches and people who respond
in concern. It serves as the metro-communications instrument
for relating all those structures which are attempting to bring
about reconciliation within the total metropolitan area.

✤✤✤ TARGET FOR MISSION

ONE OF THE GREAT WEAKNESSES of the church is to talk in general about mission but not to focus this concern on specific targets. Many years ago, when an internationally famous Boston preacher was at the height of his popularity, a newspaper reporter asked a man on the street what he thought of him. The response was, "Methinks he loves everyone in general but no one in particular." The church falls into the trap of talking about its general mission goals without zeroing in on specially designated targets.

When we consider the short-range or long-range goals of our church, we make plans out of certain stereotypes which have been developed over a period of years. We think in terms of Christian education and so channel our energies and funds through the church school; but what of those who do not attend church school? We provide a slot of time for our youth program and delegate responsibility to the minister or a dedicated lay person, but fewer and fewer young people are responding to a youth program because of the irrelevance of the church. We give our money to missions, but are haunted by the lack of personalization. So we support a missionary from "over there," or build a chapel in Nicaragua. The more affluent are even going in planeloads to visit foreign mission fields in order to get a feel for firsthand mission relationships. The money spent on one of these jaunts could support a poor family in Appalachia for a year or more, or it could provide money to build a house or rehabilitate a tenement in the slums.

We can particularize our mission by seeing it as the concern of God in the community nearby. We must look at life around us and see that the most pressing issues are poverty, the struggle of minorities, and war and peace. These are so interrelated that they defy separation or even categorizing into priorities. Yet, how much church programming revolves around these issues except in sermonizing? This is where the reconciling community comes into play. It should assume responsibility for an evangelistic or mission concern in the area of these issues. It should seek the biblical and theological bases for action. It must become the prime mover within the church structures; and if those structures hinder action, then the reconciling community should seek to change them. Let's consider the following targets for mission:

The War on Poverty

Bostonians are proud of their new Boston. It is especially typified by the changing skyline which now amazes people who see it after being away a few years. The new Government Center, the skyscraper bank buildings, and high-rise apartments are stately and impressive; but the tallest skyscrapers of all are the insurance buildings standing at the center of the city. They can be seen from every vantage point, including the distant peripheral highway Route 128. How few of the people in Boston realize, however, that at least twenty out of every one hundred people who look at those symbols of financial security and affluence do so through eyes of suffering and out of hearts of bitterness? How many of those who zip over the Southeast Expressway or who speed along the Boston Turnpike, which goes right under the foundation of one of these amazing forty-three-story structures, ever give much thought to those twenty out of one hundred who are the hidden poor of America?

When we talk about targets for mission, we find it difficult to include the poor of America. We have conceived of evangelism as searching for the lost "sheep" to share the good news of the gospel with him, but we have forgotten that being numb with hunger, cold without house heat, and burdened with bills makes it virtually impossible to hear the voice of the God of love or to believe in his personal concern. No wonder a Negro girl of eleven, who sat in a circle with other young people at a city mission camp, said she didn't believe in a personal God. She had known nothing but roach-infested housing, violence rooted in poverty, sexual incest stemming from family disintegration — and she had run away to New York three times!

The little children were herded up on the stage in the hotel ballroom. Then the president of the Women's Auxiliary made a speech to the children informing them of the generosity of the women present who were there as Christians sharing a concern for them — the poor! Then, each of the children was given a pair of mittens and a toy because Christmas was just around the corner — and now everyone would join in singing "Joy to the World, the Lord Is Come." Does it sound a little overdone? This happened, and I was the young inner-city pastor who transported those children to that significant meeting in the year of our Lord 1940. At the time I hadn't thought much about colonialism or paternalism — but I sensed it there. In the years which followed I came to understand that the goodie hand-out program at the Thanksgiving and Christmas seasons was not enough. History was to prove later that so much of this kind of Christian mission was really a salve to the conscience of those who didn't want to face the deeper causes of poverty.

Along came such men as Michael Harrington, who wrote *The Other America*. He exposed the invisible America composed of fifty million people who were hidden in the hollows of Appalachia, the ghettoes of the inner city, the tenement houses of the outer city, and even the scattered farmlands of our nation. He shocked us by making us aware of our contemporary ignorance concerning the modern poor. We had stereotyped the poor and failed to see how wrong we were. But out of this came the War on Poverty and a new era of government concern for the forgotten of the community.

Since the publishing of *The Other America* in 1962, a controversy has raged over the War on Poverty. Politicians have utilized it to become richer, and congressmen have cut its funds to prove they are in touch with the conservative, middle-class constituency at home who are afraid of the development of a welfare state. Irrespective of any government program the Christian church faces one of its most crucial hours in history in facing up to the problem of poverty. The two greatest issues facing the Christian church for the next decade are the solution of the poverty program, especially as it affects the black minority of America, and the resolution of the issue of war and peace.

Unfortunately there are all too many in the Christian church who understand the parable of the good Samaritan, who believe our Lord identified with the poor, who acknowledge the church's concern through the years for the starving of India, the unclothed of Africa, and the diseased of Latin America, but who believe the poor of America are the lazy, dirty, indolent who are just sitting around waiting for the next welfare check to arrive. Such Christians have not realized the theological and biblical implications of contemporary poverty. So often their lack of sensitivity is the result of not knowing what it is to be maimed in body and spirit, living at the animal level with no hope for the future. They have never sat in a slum tenement and talked with a mother whose baby was bitten by a rat! They have never agonized with children whose mother in a weakened condition fell down a staircase and was killed because she was giving her food to her seven children while attempting as a widow to keep that family together and going! They have not known what it is to be so dehumanized that God seems far away or dead! These are reasons why the war on poverty is not the government's burden alone; it is the church's also! This is why the Christian community has got to establish contact with the community organizations which are attempting to do something to bring about a radical transformation of American society.

Many of the so-called intelligent middle-class churchmen of the United States are utterly ignorant about the poverty question. Because they have been raised in an environment which looks upon the free-enterprise system as the door to plenty for all, they have been slow to realize this is not so. Because they have been suspicious of big government and the creeping trend toward socialism, they have fought government programs which express concern for people caught in social mouse traps. But there is a growing awareness that man's responsibility to man can be expressed through government and the social order. It was once held that Social Security and Medicare would never come to America, but they did. A nation great enough to put men on the moon must also eliminate conditions which obscure the sun of full living from deprived people.

Humanization of Minorities

Three black members of the Los Angeles Black Congress faced an audience in the ballroom of a Washington hotel. One hundred urban workers from major cities in the United States had been called together to face the issues of urban tensions and the Black Congress men were there to help the group sense the mood of the Afro-American, to listen to what he was trying to say.

"We're sick and tired of the line you religious frauds have been dishing out to us blacks," they said. "We're sick and tired of this Jesus stuff which has been used as a tranquilizer to keep the black community in slavery for 300 years. But we've learned from you — we've become good Americans; and good Americans always solve their problems through violence — and that's our plan, man, to burn this country down!"

This particular conference was one of many held to establish dialogue with the Negro community. But the Negro rightfully declares he is sick and tired of dialogue; he wants action! So do people all around this world; the poor are determined to rise above their limited level of life; the dispossessed are determined to possess what they have been denied; the dehumanized are seeking ways to become human beings — and they will pay any price to gain this right. They have nothing to lose but their chains.

The chief issue of the emerging twenty-first century is humanization for all men. The Christian community must develop tactics which focus on this crucial problem at every level of relationship. Christians must give prime attention to the Black Power struggle, understanding it and readjusting their thinking to affirm the reality and authenticity of the quest of the blacks for dignity. Basic to Christian tactics is listening, learning, and loving. We cannot close our ears to a Stokely Carmichael, however much we disagree or are shocked by what he says. We must tune in open, consecrated minds to hear the voices in the major urban centers of America. We must remember that black people now hold the balance of electoral power in some of the largest cities of our nation. Population trends make it clear that in the next few years Black America will make up the majority in a dozen or more key cities. In Washington, D.C., and Newark, New

Jersey, they are now a majority. In Cleveland, Ohio, and Gary, Indiana, they have elected Negro mayors. In Detroit, Baltimore, and St. Louis they represent one-third of the population; in Oakland, Cincinnati, Chicago, and Philadelphia they now constitute one-fourth. In other words, the white man, who too often sees only the power of numbers, had better realize that twenty-five million blacks are themselves now aware of a new strength in numbers and experience a new hope through political organizations; and there is no power more forceful than that which suddenly receives new spirit through hope.

At the previously mentioned meeting in Washington, the Black Churchmen met in a black caucus and issued the following statement:

> We, Black Churchmen, meeting in caucus find ourselves profoundly distressed, disturbed, frustrated, and in a state of utter disquietude about a nature and mission of the church in a time of revolution. We have come to realize that Black Power is an expression of the need for Black Authenticity in a white-dominated society, a society which has from its earliest beginnings displayed unadulterated racism. We affirm without fear of repudiation the meaningfulness of blackness and our identity as Black Churchmen. We confess the guilt which is ours for past actions and inaction in failing to be instruments for the expression of the will of God as Black Churchmen. We therefore propose now to speak and act, out of our own shame and guilt, concerning the lack of the Church's responsiveness to the needs of black people seeking to be free and human in a dehumanizing world. . . .
>
> We further call upon the white churches to commit themselves to the following:
>
> (1) To join with us in affirming the legitimacy of the Black Power movement and to be open to the word that God is speaking to us through the issues it raises.
>
> (2) To turn in their distress to the leadership of the Black Church recognizing the insights borne out of a history of struggle against the exclusion and oppression of Black people in Church and Society; supporting the initiatives borne of these insights; and seeking the guidance, collaboration and support of the Black

Churches in the formulation and implementation of all church policies and programs.

(3) To declare a three-year moratorium on suburban new church development, and make the funds available from such work in people-centered ministries in the Black and White communities.[1]

This statement of the Black Churchmen is typical of what the Afro-American is saying, but the problem lies in the responses of bafflement and ignorance which come from the white Christian community. Many refuse to believe that they have been colonialistic or paternalistic toward the black. Perhaps the most confused is the liberal churchman who has demonstrated, marched, been imprisoned, and as far as he can see it, has been completely color-blind. He has, in his own thinking, made a total identification with the black, and now he feels rejected and hurt.

Dr. Alvin F. Poussaint, assistant professor of psychiatry at Tufts University Medical College, was responsible for an interesting article in *Ebony* magazine entitled, "How the 'White Problem' Spawned 'Black Power.'" In the article, which was based on a paper which he read before the American Psychiatric Association, he shared some of the thinking of young blacks from Hattiesburg, Mississippi, who openly expressed opinions about civil rights workers who went South to work side by side with the blacks in lunch-counter integration causes and voter registration.[2]

Many of the young blacks felt that the whites who went South were doing so out of a need for self-aggrandizement and self-glorification. The blacks looked upon this as a messianic, white-superiority role which they called the "white African queen complex" and the "Tarzan" complex. They claimed they were bossed around by the well-meaning whites.

[1] "A Declaration of Black Churchmen," a statement developed at the NCC Conference on the Church and Urban Tension, Washington, D.C., September, 1967.

[2] Alvin F. Poussaint, "How the 'White Problem' Spawned 'Black Power,'" *Ebony*, August, 1967, p. 88.

But the whites who apparently did the most harm were the long-haired, bearded characters who gave the black the impression they were identifying more effectively with the black community by being dirty and unkempt. They gave the impression they were "getting down to the level of the people," but this merely angered local Negroes and filled them with contempt.

But the Civil Rights movement of that level and character is all over! The white liberal will no longer be able to assuage his conscience with this kind of identification; in fact the black community is telling him to turn toward white suburbia and bring about the changes needed there.

If the white liberal has been at fault in his unconscious manifestation of paternalism, the white conservative also stands under judgment for his refusal to lift a finger to open the gate of freedom for the black. All too many of the vast majority of pious, religious Americans fall in this category. They have been captive to the myths which have been created concerning the black. They have actually believed he was an inferior animal, a minstrel-show entertainer who could bring laughs, or a physical specimen who would win boxing bouts, Olympic gold medals, and football trophies. But when it came down to running cities, Congress, or even the White House, the religious white man and woman sincerely believed in the false image of the Negro passed on to them by a blind generation. They expressed concern when riots broke out; why couldn't the Negro lift himself up by the bootstrap and improve his lot? Wasn't he the dirty, ignorant human being who threw garbage in the alleys, allowed his tenement house to be run down, and made it unsafe for people to walk the streets of the inner city?

The farmers of North Dakota and the suburbanites of Wellesley Hills all felt that good old American initiative would solve everything. They had no idea of the organized power structures which created insurmountable conditions, of a poverty culture which had forced a way of life upon a people; saddest of all, those who bore the name of Christ really didn't see how this problem was related to the mission of the church. They gave money every Sunday to support the mission cause in Africa, Japan, or Latin America, but could not conceive of the Christian community's participation in the Black Revolution.

But times are changing; and now, even though late, there are those who sincerely desire to offer themselves to this cause. How can they move? What suggestion can be made to enable the local church or religious community to become the channel of God's spirit and his will in facing this most crucial issue in modern society? I would suggest a tactical plan based on four words: Information, Invitation, Coalition, Participation.

Let's consider these:

Information: Because the communications gap is so great between the black and white communities the Christian church has a responsibility for closing it. This can be done by forming a reconciling community in a local church or among a group of local churches charged with the concern for communicating the new image of the Negro to the white constituency. This group might be a study group willing to read, absorb, and analyze the latest Black Power literature, whether the biography of Malcolm X, or writings of Carmichael or Fanon. A subscription to black newspapers like *Muhammad Speaks* (the Black Muslim periodical) or *Ebony* magazine (the middle-class Negro counterpart to *Life* magazine) would open up resources for hearing the black voice. Studies might be made of African history and culture as they relate to the Afro-American. Most of all the group would try to understand the statement of the militant young black who said, "Our trouble is that Martin Luther King has been telling us to love others before we have learned to love ourselves."

Then the most significant thing that a concerned group would do is communicate this information to the white church.

A thorough job of reeducation concerning the Negro must be done from the ground up. It must be done in the church school with the youngest children who are being culturally deprived of the privilege of knowing the black community. It must be taken into the public schools, into the homes, into the business sector, and into the political arena. This is the awesome task of the Christian white church for the future!

Invitation: This is the difficult word because it means waiting with patience for an invitation that may not come in our lifetime. But it means standing back and waiting to be invited *by the black community* to enter *into their* community *according to their rules and standards!* But the invitation will come; it will come as a reversal of trends to integrate blacks into white neighborhoods. It will require moving into inner-city ghettoes to learn about and submit to the Negro culture as a superior and beneficial way of life. It may be an invitation to participate in the manifestations of revolution which will not be pleasant to accept, but may be the crucial test! Certainly there will be invitations to participate in pooling knowledge in business affairs, community organization, church matters, but again according to the dictates of the black community!

Coalition: Invitation leads to coalition. The American black is very suspicious of coalitions because he has been at the bottom of the pile when such relationships have been formed. He knows that the most liberal white is dominated by a white-controlled society which, innocently or not, thinks white in all it does. To the black this means when you talk about a coalition you ask big business to put money in a ghetto, and new buildings arise. But the black is still the recipient of the "plantation owners'" goodness, and the white business investor becomes richer at the expense of the black. This is not the kind of coalition the black wants. He believes the next significant coalition in his history is that between the poor blacks and the poor whites. This could become a major instrument for change in the innards of American society. However, the poor white is more often than not hostile to the poor black. He is even more threatened by him than his white suburban cousin. The white Christian community faces a challenge in educating the poor white for coalition on the black man's terms — and this will not be easy!

Participation: The major participation of the white Christian community for the future will be financial participation. There's one difficulty, however. Who wants to support a revolution against himself? Yet, we must run this risk. Money must be made available to the black community with no strings attached. Some major denominations are now doing this. More must follow.

How can one learn self-government with pride and freedom unless he is given the right of failure? Has any young nation including the United States been totally mature in its handling of money? Was an Irish Boston under the leadership of Mayor James Michael Curley any more responsible for its financial expenditures than a black ghetto seeking to learn how to manage its own internal affairs? The white community must be willing to trust the black community and give it the money to build its own apartments, manage its own banks, and sell its own food. Out of this kind of coalition of trust will come a new relationship which will create the kind of community in America all men have hoped for. So, white Christians must play a supportive role, holding themselves ready to respond to the invitation to participate in a task which has at its heart concern for people as people.

Achieving a Peaceful World

Five young men stand at the altar of the West End Church and burn their draft cards in a silver urn held by a minister of the gospel. Members of that church are shocked to see this on the six o'clock television news program. Some rejoice because their church is in the news doing something about a controversial issue. Others are dismayed that a seemingly unpatriotic act took place in their holy sanctuary. The continuing battle between the traditionalists and the experimentalists rages over whether anti-war demonstrations are the business of the church or an effrontery to the state. Tragically enough the traditionalists in this case are the adults, and the experimentalists are the youth of our nation. The adults have been conditioned to accept a war-psychology way of life, but the youth, stimulated by college professors and mass media, have challenged this psychology. The adults have a vested interest in war because their bread and butter depends upon it. The young people have a natural desire for peace because their school chums die in Vietnam and they fail to grasp the logic which demands young death!

The middle-aged of the world today ought to be ardent pacifists! They were born in the wake of World War I and saw the tremendous film entitled "All's Quiet on the Western Front," which brought a strong indictment against war. Then they were thrust into the holocaust of World War II. At that time there was no choice but to destroy Hitler and to respond to the bombing of Pearl Harbor by the Japanese. But later involvements in Korea and Vietnam have done nothing more than build new walls between nations and peoples. Possession of the Bomb by key nations, including Red China, makes it more imperative than ever that American leaders rethink the nation's role in determining the future of smaller nations. And now after fifty years of wars, declared and undeclared, the church of Jesus Christ finds that it is losing its hold on youth because they want to live in a peaceful world! Young people cannot understand their middle-aged parents who seem to have docilely accepted war and tragically carry on business as usual without making affirmative moves to educate the Christian church to become an influence for peace.

These same young people know why those involved in the poverty war are concerned about military war. The billions of dollars spent on war could win the war against poverty. The Negro young person is too often the one who gives his life at the distant front! And most of all, the very acquiescent spirit which made the state church so impotent in Hitler's day has become typical of American churches. We cannot preach about the Prince of Peace and pour bombs on villages — regardless of the reason! Unless the church enters into a totally relevant program of teaching for peace, it will be completely forsaken by the youth of this and coming generations.

Like the weather, everyone talks about war and the danger of nuclear annihilation but no one does much to alleviate the threat. However the Reverend Harriet B. Kurtz, who is a minister in the United Church of Christ, has been commissioned by the Board of Homeland Ministries of her denomination to work as a missioner in the area of war prevention. With her husband, Howard G. Kurtz, a former Lieutenant Colonel in the United States Air Force, she is presenting a plan which attempts to face this issue of war in a Christian and practical way. They call it GLOBAL COMPASSIONATE POWER. It is directed to the "dove" and the "hawk" with the purpose of developing a system of Global Safety Power which would bring arms, nuclear weapons, armies, and navies under an international body related to the United Nations.

There is no question but what the United Nations has been rendered powerless because it has been set up as a city government over the new world-city, while the same world-city police force has been divided into autonomous units.

The Kurtz proposal is that this Global Safety System be set up by the nations of the world with authority to take action as a unit. At present when two nations come into conflict with each other, there is no way to mobilize physical or moral forces to prevent the conflict from spreading. In calling for this kind of international police force in the new world-city in which we live, the Kurtz plan suggests that it have three major functions:

1. Intelligence — the immediate detection of the presence of danger.

2. Operations — the authority to move promptly to the scene to investigate and to prevent the escalation of any war-like activity.

3. Planning — the responsibility of developing contingent plans to meet future problems as they develop.

They suggest the Global Safety Authority have an Aerospace Force, Marine Force, and Land Force. These would be financed and manned by all the nations together.

With increasing problems created by the invasion of space and the stockpiling of nuclear weapons, this suggested procedure makes sense. It seeks through the full participation of all nations to solve the police problems of the world while maintaining peace among all nations.

This plan is submitted as one practical type of thinking which is going on today concerning the issues of war and peace. The Christian church may reject this particular plan entirely, but it cannot escape its responsibility for making peace one of the targets for mission as it seeks to establish a world community based upon the directives of God's Word.

Violence as a Way of Life

While this book was being written, it was interrupted by two tragic and senseless assassinations. First, Dr. Martin Luther King, Jr., was gunned down by a sniper in Memphis, Tennessee, and then Senator Robert F. Kennedy was shot in Los Angeles, California. After each of these events Americans asked themselves, "Are we a sick nation? Why do these things happen?"

There is no one simple explanation for the acts of insane individuals, but one thing is certain: our nation has developed a sub-culture of violence! Our people spend so many hours watching stabbings, shootings, bombings, and other forms of brutality on the television and theater screen that they have become totally identified with the glorification of violence. Our parks and national shrines are covered with statues of men who, out of patriotism and self-sacrifice, were forced to resort to violence. Our parades are made up primarily of soldiers, sailors, and marines; opportunities for showing symbols of peace and love are rare.

In contrast to our culture, Norway's parks and public places have statues glorifying life and beauty. I watched a five-hour parade on their Day of Independence and did not see one military unit, or gun, or rocket in it. Instead there were school children carrying flags of the nation, bands playing gay marching music, and the teachers from all the schools and universities. They were parading the pride of their nation as a symbol of peace through education.

Let no one misunderstand me. I am not saying that we should disband armies or neglect our war heroes. But I am saying we have so elevated the violent aspects of our history that the gun-toting Westerner (the good guy in the white hat) and even the Bonnie and Clyde characters (the bad guys who evoke our sympathy) have become such a part of our unconsciousness that we have lost our sensitivity to the value of human life.

The whole question of violence is related to a nation's regard for people. Because of population growth, mobility, technology, urbanization, and the stress on individuality we have developed a common disregard for people. This is demonstrated by traffic brutality, litterbug indifference, and crowd domination of the person. Some of the common courtesies, which are seen in England where people queue up at the bus depots, are seldom observed in America; and the quality of citizenship as manifested by the cleanliness of so many European cities where individuals scrub their streets because of their pride and their concern for others has been lost in America.

The United States way of life is still influenced by the

pioneer concept of competition, while the more mature European way has learned cooperation. Americans have glorified power: the football hero stands above the professor; the ruthless business man stands above the humble social worker.

The reconciling community has a unique role to play in revealing the misuses of power which are new forms of hidden violence. We have decried the assassination of great leaders while we have destroyed the humanity of the little people with systems based upon war, power, and ruthless competition. We have assumed that violence was an individual matter and now realize that it is a corporate way of life which can only be dealt with by a society which develops a sense of Christian community.

You Name the Target

I have suggested that the key issues of our day — poverty, race, war, violence — are some targets for mission. They are not the only issues, but they embrace most of the key problems which face us as the Christian community. Problems of the aging, traffic safety, youth, the sexual revolution, and a long list of other concerns which emerge from our world might be added to the list.

Each of us responds to targets according to his background, his culture, and his religious heritage. Each one must face the questions: Do I have a target for mission? Am I seeking a way to involvement? Is my commitment real because it is dynamic? The answers will determine the effectiveness of each person's life as a witness and participant in God's world.

✤✤✤ THE RECONCILING COMMUNITY: AGENTS OF RECONCILIATION

THE NEWSPAPER HEADLINE told about a man entering a factory and proceeding to shoot down a number of surprised and helpless fellow employees. Subsequent articles in the newspapers and national periodicals pointed out that this man was emotionally disturbed and had deep psychological problems. Even though many people had seen the signs of his emotional sickness, he had no one to whom he could turn. This lonely man epitomizes urban man lost in the midst of the masses of people who are faceless, nameless, and apparently uninterested in him. In the play, *The Roar of the Greasepaint — the Smell of the Crowd,* Cocky sings a song entitled, "Who Can I Turn To?"

> Who can I turn to when nobody needs me?
> My heart wants to know and so I must go
> Where destiny leads me.
> With no star to guide me, and no-one beside me,

115

> I'll go on my way, and after the day,
> The darkness will hide me;
> And may-be tomorrow I'll find what I'm after —
> I'll throw off my sorrow, beg steal or borrow
> My share of laughter.
> With you I could learn to, —
> With you on a new day, —
> But who can I turn to if you turn away.[1]

Much is being written and said these days about human relationships in the urbanized, technological society. Many people are still following the old line about the hostility of the city. Most preachers have been guilty of citing stories concerning the girl raped in the alley, the woman knifed in the doorway, the car entrapped in a flood, while others looked on in apparent indifference and with apparent hardheartedness. They have talked about the depersonalization of man in the urban world and have attempted to communicate the fact that for the city dweller the person-to-person relationship is almost impossible to establish. There may be some justification for this attitude, but it has been overemphasized. The truth is that the very existence of the city, which shoves people close together in a crowded elevator or subway train, which makes them walk together in crowds at the shopping center, which packs them in the high-rise apartment house or the office building, really brings people closer to each other. But the sheer complexity of the life in which these people find themselves enmeshed paradoxically enough deepens their dependence on each other and yet overwhelms them so that they do not know how to establish the simple life and love relationships which have been known throughout the history of mankind. For example, how does one love his neighbor when

[1] "Who Can I Turn To (When Nobody Needs Me)" from the musical production *The Roar of the Greasepaint — the Smell of the Crowd*, Words and Music by Leslie Bricusse and Anthony Newley TRO © Copyright 1964 Concord Music Ltd., London, England. All publication rights controlled by Musical Comedy Productions, Inc., New York, for the U.S.A. and Canada. Used by permission.

the neighbor may not want to be loved? Or does one love his neighbor who does not understand him, and is not even able to communicate with him because of a language or culture barrier?

Yet, who can I turn to when nobody needs me? My heart does want to know — to know some of the answers about life and death, sin and forgiveness, and the basic values for discovering the key to happy living. One thing is certain; the person who hangs onto the subway train strap beside me, or who hustles past me on the street, or who sits with that frustrated anguished look in a traffic tie-up has all of the same basic, spiritual needs that man has always had. However, whereas man once turned toward his minister, or priest, or rabbi, now he can't distinguish the man of God from the others. Whereas once the simple, uncomplicated way of life made it possible for one or two of the key members of the little local church to be available in special ways, today these people are lost in the crowd.

The popularity of radio talk programs which can be found around the clock demonstrates something of this need for human contacts. During the long night hours, the moderator of the program inevitably asks the question, "Why are you up at this hour of the night?" The answers that come back are varied: "I just got in from work," or "I'm going to work," or "I couldn't sleep," or sometimes, quite frankly, "I felt like talking to someone." Everyone needs to talk to somebody. Everybody needs to turn to somebody. The Christian community must provide that opportunity by training its constituency to learn how to listen to those who want to talk. The technique in the past has been to talk and then listen for results. Today's society demands listening but to the listening must be added the word of healing, of forgiveness, of comfort, and of illumination. We members of the Christian church are a priesthood of believers who have a responsibility toward those around us. This is our mission of reconciliation.

Back to the Curbstone

Beverly and Daffy walked along one of the narrow streets on a stifling, hot summer day in the North End of the city. They were carrying an orange crate filled with an assortment of children's games. Coming to a group of children who looked as though they didn't know what to do with themselves in this crowded area, the girls sat down on a curbstone and proceeded to take the games out on the sidewalk. The children watched them carefully, and then coming closer asked about the games. Within moments these children, who were ordinarily hostile to outsiders and suspicious of adults in general, were sitting on that same curbstone playing games with the girls. In time some of the mothers, hanging out of the tenement windows, inquired about what was taking place down on the sidewalk. When they discovered that these children, who are generally harassed by the police and ignored by the average adult, were playing with two college girls who were there out of commitment and concern, the mothers joined them. They brought chairs with them and insisted that the girls sit in the chairs while they served cookies. But the rapport and relationship which had developed between the girls and the children immediately disappeared when the girls left the curbstone and sat in the chairs. They were now called "Miss" as though they were school teachers. The relationship they had on the curbstone was no longer there. So, these girls thanked the mothers for the chairs and sat down close to the children, having a marvelous afternoon, treating them as human beings, giving of themselves as children to children.

One of the things learned from this kind of experience is that if there is such a distance between the curbstone and the chair for two young ladies who walk into the midst of the teeming city out of Christian concern, how much greater is the distance between that curbstone and the pew, or a Sunday school table, or a baptismal font, or communion table.

This experience shows that in the current age Christians must find ways to get back to the curbstone. They do not have to compromise their position, their way of life, or their conviction; but they must be willing to discard all of the things which come between them and other persons. Also, they need to learn how to move out into new forms of ministry which will make reconciliation possible. For example, one suburban church rented a storefront in another part of the community in order that youth who would not come to the church but who would enter a coffee house might establish a relationship with the youth of the church. Still another church turned over a house which had been providing rental income to become a center for such curbstone relationships.

Archie Hargraves, director of Metropolitan Mission at the Urban Training Center in Chicago, writes about a group of United Church of Christ ministers and laymen from Los Angeles and its suburbs who have attempted to face the racial crisis of that area by implementing a plan designated as "Metropolitan Time Tellers."

Each congregation of the churches involved has been asked to release five of its key laymen from involvement in the life in the church for a period of six months. These laymen are to continue in their regular occupations and in their normal family life, but the time they usually give to their local congregation is to be redirected into a mission of reconciliation.

In addition, each congregation has been asked to release at least five other laymen who are acutely sensitive and troubled about the state and condition of the institutional church and yet are not very actively involved in the local congregation's life. They would come from that peripheral group which, as has been mentioned previously, exists in most congregations. This is that group of very critical, creative, imaginative people who perhaps have given up the institutional church because it has traditionally been a place of compromise, caution, and comfort.

This group of agents of reconciliation from the local congregations (the time tellers) are "regathered" at a central point in the inner city for training, discussion, briefing, orientation, and exposure concerning the Negro in American life. They seek out ways by which they can relate directly with the issues, the needs, and the people in this time of crisis.

Under the guidance of the Reverend Reuben Sheares, the minister for Metropolitan Mission, the time tellers meet (for the first time in their lives) Negroes who are no longer their inferiors or servants but who come to them as equals with equal aspirations. Together they seek out ways to look at the inner city and at suburbia. Together they seek out ways to make relevant and redemptive their style of life across racial and socio-economic barriers. They come to grips with questions of the assignment of Negro ministers to new churches in suburbia without regard to race, or of making available more job opportunities through the financial centers of the city. Something of this same kind of approach is being made across the country through a national movement known as the Urban Coalition in which businessmen of importance from the power structures of city life may carry out their Christian conviction by establishing relationships with the dispossessed in this time of revolution.

The Reverend Mr. Hargraves writes,

> The Time Tellers will aim to help the church, as the mode of transmission for the gospel, find renewal in this particular time and in specific places as it is confronted by specific situations, so that it will be the conscience of the metropolis and make an appreciable difference in the metropolitan style of behavior.[2]

Rebellious Youth

All heads in the congregation turned as the returning college student sought his place in the church congregation. He was

[2] Archie Hargraves, "Metropolitan Time Tellers," *The City Church*, May-June, 1964, p. 5.

home from college over the holiday weekend, but those who remembered him as the clean-shaven, starry-eyed, young man who was sent off to the college campus, now whispered to each other as they shared their dismay and disappointment over his long hair and beard. Rebellious youth are doing what youth have done through all ages — attempting to cut those ties between themselves and the adults who dominate them. Because the current and contemporary rebellion seems to be accentuated through the mass media, it appears that there is a wider gulf between the adult world and the young people than ever before. On high school and college campuses there are signs of great distrust of the adult world. Attempts to keep chemical company officials from interviewing students, the blocking of the path of military officials as they attempt to recruit, and the downright indifference to the campus chaplain and church; all bring responses of fear and perplexity within the breasts of parents. Adults might understand what is taking place if they would listen more closely to the music that is being sung by the mod artists who are expressing the despair and skepticism of contemporary youth. Singers like Bob Dylan, for example, are attempting to express what is really going on in the world compared to what is being *taught about* what is going on in the world. Contemporary singers are expressing the deep skepticism about the adult who at Christmas time sings about peace on earth, good will among men, and yet is completely dependent upon the military way of solving the problems in the international world.

What has happened is that in this scientific age we have taught our children to search for truth and find it, regardless of the results; and as they have taken these scientific methodologies and applied them to all of life, they have discovered that adults have built a mythological world. We have taught them good things about farm life and yet have not shared anything of the terribly pressing problems of the misery of those in Appalachia. But they have discovered this for themselves. We have taught them about the city but we have not brought them up to date on the most serious of city problems relating to the poverty-stricken and the racially disenfranchised. Also, in regard to sex we have taught them some ideals about sex life which have been utterly discredited by the attitudes expressed in novels, movies, and television. They have discovered that our words have said one thing and our lives have manifested another. Hypocrisy stands out as the key to this disillusionment of youth, particularly with the Christian church.

Illustrative of this attitude is the presentation made by a group of young people in a church worship service on Youth Sunday. Three of these young people, in speaking to the congregation, shared some of the thinking of the youth world which even parents do not hear very often. They explained why the church was having problems with the traditional approach to youth in the community and why so many young people are leaving the church. One of the speakers startled the congregation by spelling out why young people are turning their backs on the traditional, institutional church. She said that the church is made up of phonies; the young people do not believe in the kind of God who is being presented to them; the knowledge and faith of the church are dying — and, she added, because of its comforts, the church is the haven of the frightened and the weak. Now, these are pretty strong words, and the adults were not overly happy with this kind of analysis of their own spiritual health condition. Lack of understanding between parents and children is not unique with this generation, but the very means of communication, the complexity and speed of contemporary life, and the openness and rationale of a technological and scientific age have made the lack more vivid than ever before in history.

In all fairness to these young people, they also noted the positive side; they stressed that they believed in the church because it is God's and not just man's; they affirmed the church because whatever value judgments on matters of race, sex, and war they have today, the church has given them. What they have learned about morals and ethics has come primarily through the church, they said, adding: "We think our children still need this, and we ask you to understand us and them as we seek to become in reality the church." Another of the speakers reminded the young people of the fact that they are not the youth department *of the church* but are *the church* and in the words of one of these young men, "We are the church with you born anew in Christ and seeking to join him in his mission in his world."

Let no one be discouraged about how our youth think. On the contrary, some of the most meaningful movements in the world are taking place under the inspiration, guidance, and leadership of enlightened youth. But because the twenty-first century will soon see that 50 percent or more of the American population will be twenty-one years of age and under, the church has a great responsibility to strengthen the moral and spiritual fiber of this generation and the next.

Reaching the Happy Pagan

There is a renewed interest in the meaning of conversion these days. In conferences held around the world major denominations are discovering that this issue comes to the fore whenever men try anew to analyze and understand the contemporary implications of the teachings of Jesus Christ — he who said: "Except you become converted and become as little children you shall not enter the kingdom of heaven."

The happy, comfortable pagan who has no fear of spending an eternity in hell, any more than he has of a drought cutting the food supply in his freezer, is the man who needs converting. In the midst of his affluence and busyness he is not crying out, "How shall I be saved?" To the contrary, he couldn't care less about being saved as he makes his way to the bank with his earthly savings! He is concerned only about how he can make more money, how he can acquire more things, how he can be more comfortable. Some religious leaders have been of the opinion that all one has to do is wait for that moment of crisis when such people will fall upon their knees and cry out to God. Sometimes this does happen, but more often the questions asked in a time of crisis are: Where can I find a good doctor? What pill can I take? What world can I escape into? Or what good travel agent would you recommend?

A new missionary to a foreign field may assume that everybody has a hunger within his heart for Jesus. Often he finds that this is not so! For example, in the rural areas of Mexico many of those living out of wedlock were a very happy people. I found that those who liked to drink pulque and escape into a world of fantasy on their own lost weekends were a happy and contented people. The argument that this is not real happiness is hard to substantiate. When a person, living in sin (which means having several wives, or stealing to make ends meet) "comes to Jesus," his eyes are not miraculously opened to the necessity of marrying one of the wives or giving up his stealing. He must determine which wife he will marry and what obligation he has to the other women in his life. I discovered, as a missionary or lay evangelist teaches a new ethic about the questions of marriage or of honesty, that eventually these answers are learned but not as a natural consequence of the experience of conversion.

Two observations about the conversion experience may be seen in this example from Mexico. First, this conversion experience must be passed from one person to another. This is such a common, simple truth that it seems superfluous to mention it, and yet how many Christians of today really feel that they have a responsibility to share the good news in order that complete change might take place in another person? The second thing is that conversion comes through the communication of truth. It is not enough to say "Come to Jesus." There must be communication of what the consequences of that coming mean. The generation of a desire to know God through the living Christ and the communication of the responsibilities of relating to that living Christ must go hand in hand. In the modern world conversion has become a topic rarely discussed in the average local church because of this generation's reaction to the pietism of the past where the experience was generated but the responsibilities were not communicated.

The presence of Christ in human life affirms man's acceptance of himself as he is, because Christ affirms the acceptance by God of every kind of man. Christian experience also means the acceptance of others as they are, because it affirms the acceptance by God of others as they are. Conversion is the opening of human life to this acceptance of oneself, of his fellowman, and of God.

Conversion is the act of reconciliation between a real person and his false self; it is the act of reconciliation between a real person and others. All too often in the past, conversion has meant only man reconciled to God, but God does not want a man on such limited terms. This is what the "death of God" theologians are trying to say. God has put a barrier between himself and man as a temporary measure to force man to come on God's terms! God wants man as he is — not as a phony all dressed up in his Sunday best with pious phrases on his lips! God wants man as he is, regardless of his dress, haircut, language, problems, weaknesses, strengths, and dreams. God wants man as he is, confessing his frailty and accepting the love which God offers. He wants man as the reconciled and the reconciling.

In his first letter John wrote:

> We know and to some extent realize the love of God for us because Christ expressed it in laying down his life for us. We must in turn express our love by laying down our lives for those who are our brothers. But as for the well-to-do man who sees his brother in want but shuts his eyes — and his heart — how could anyone believe that

the love of God lives in him? My children, let us love not merely in theory or in words — let us love in sincerity and in practice!

(1 John 3:16-18) [3]

John is communicating the truth about real conversion. If a man has truly been changed by the presence of Christ in his life, his eyes will be open to the needs within himself and he will make relationships right! His true, split self will become whole, and the experience of forgiveness will be his.

While returning from Europe on the S. S. *Leonardo da Vinci*, I was invited to lead the Protestant worship service. Many persons who were fleeing the Middle East crisis between Israel and Egypt were on board the ship and attended the service.

I had invited a lovely Christian couple from Egypt, who were migrating to Canada, to provide the music for the service. Mr. and Mrs. Albert Saif, both Arabs, were Presbyterians who talked and lived their Christian faith. She played the piano and he sang a solo during the service.

At the close of the worship time an American woman from Libya approached the Saifs and said, "I've got a confession to make to you. When I saw you playing the piano at the beginning of the service, I wanted to get up and walk out. You see, my husband is an American oil executive in Libya and I was forced to flee for my life because of the Arabs who stoned our house, attacked our car, and drove us out of the country. We loved the Arabs for eight years; we did everything we could to treat them right, and now they've done this to us! I got on this ship filled with hatred toward all Arabs! And then I saw you this morning! But as you played and sang I knew I couldn't be a child of God and go on with this hatred! I had to come and ask your forgiveness."

The tears flowed and arms embraced as people from differ-

[3] *The New Testament in Modern English*, © J. B. Phillips 1958. Used by permission of The Macmillan Company and Geoffrey Bles Ltd.

ent backgrounds and cultures were reconciled in Christ. A little Christian community was drawn together for a few days on that big ship!

Reconciliation between individuals is one of the goals of the reconciling community. Every technique and method known to the church and the world must be applied to this end. This is the individual application of the gospel's implications. This is the traditional approach of the church to mankind's needs. This American woman now had new responsibilities toward finding reconciliation between the Arab and non-Arab world. These would lead to involvement in politics, business systems, and other systems which perpetuate separation.

But there is also the matter of collective reconciliation! All of us live in complicated structures which tend to separate us from our brothers. Our eyes are closed to the needs of others by systems which act as walls between us. We all live in ghettos of one kind or another — suburban, inner-city, small-town, or even rural! We are naturally attracted to those who are most like us and repelled by those who do not know or understand us. The responsibility of the Christian community is to smash ghettoism in American church and community life. Though we all tend to resist this, the church has the responsibility to force us outward into the larger world where we can become the agents of reconciliation.

At a meeting of ministers in an inner-city black ghetto there were guests present — some community organization men, council of churches representatives, and the captain of the local police station. When the white police captain of this all-black community was presented, he spoke to the group asking for their cooperation in fighting crime on the streets. One of the angry young blacks asked for an opportunity to respond. He and two other non-ministerial guests then proceeded to speak to this police captain. They poured out their hearts as they spoke of police brutality and the activity of police officers during the riot of a past summer. They showed shocking hatred toward the police department and the one who represented it. They flatly rejected his blanket offer of protection for their community and accused him of actually being their prison guard on behalf of the white community which had created the black ghetto.

How can reconciliation be achieved within this community? What is the role of the black ministers who were gathered at that meeting? What is my role? What is the role of the white churches? It is not enough to talk in generalities about love and reconciliation as though each were a pill which one takes at church on Sunday morning. A responsible, concerned group of spiritually motivated people must find ways to bring about communication and relationships between the alienated. This may mean dealing directly with the mayor or the governor of the state. It may mean gathering special funds which will be turned over to ghetto areas for the purpose of self-determination in business, education, and home. It may mean cutting back on the utilization of funds in suburban and rural areas for the sake of those who rebel out of bitterness and hatred after so many years of injustice and suffering. The gathered community of Jesus Christ will become revolutionaries in the true sense of the word as they attempt to destroy those social and cultural structures which have tended to separate brother from brother. This may not be the traditional approach of the church to mankind's needs, but it is evangelism of the highest order because it establishes community and prepares the way for the true coming of our Lord.

The world is waiting for the Christian church to combine its great historical and traditional forces with the insights of the contemporary world in order that the purpose of the coming of our Lord Jesus Christ might have meaning for the age in which we live.